Terrific Trickster Tales from Asia

Cathy Spagnoli

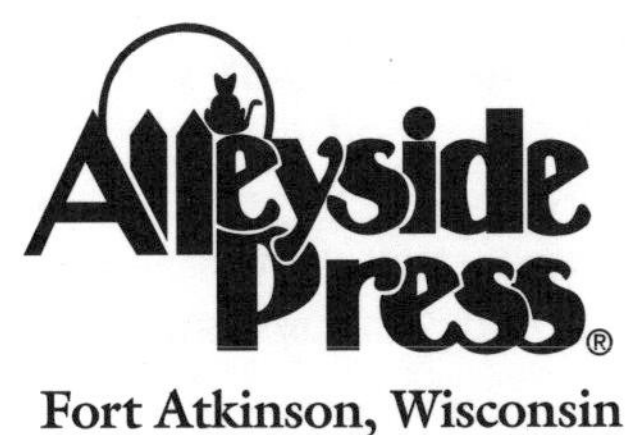

Fort Atkinson, Wisconsin

Published by Alleyside Press, an imprint of Highsmith Press
Highsmith Press
W5527 Highway 106
P.O. Box 800
Fort Atkinson, Wisconsin 53538-0800
1-800-558-2110
hpress@highsmith.com
www.hpress.highsmith.com

Cover design: Debra Neu Sletten

The paper used in this publication meets the minimum requirements of American National Standard for Information Science — Permanence of Paper for Printed Library Material. ANSI/NISO Z39.48-1992.

Contents

Part 3: More Ideas and Resources

Part 1

On Storytelling and Tricksters

Beginning with Tricksters

Everyone loves a trickster, except the one being tricked! Tricksters are common in almost all times and almost all countries. The trickster tales in this book are from Asia, but many of the tricks are familiar, for tricksters around the world share common aims. Tricksters fight injustice, teach kings and rulers, outwit monsters and those in authority, solve cases and problems, and just have fun.

Often, tricksters are physically weak, small, poor, young, or from a lower class, yet they outwit those much more powerful, rich, or strong. Listeners of all cultures seem to enjoy this reversal of the usual; it keeps their spirits up.

Tricksters come in all shapes and forms, and in large numbers around the world. There are tricky humans like Hershele of Ostropol from the Jewish tradition, High John the Conqueror from African-American lore, or Pedro de Urdemalas from Mexico. There are witty scholars and judges like Judge Ooka of Japan, Trang Quyenh of Vietnam, or Princess Learned-in-the-Law from Burma. And, of course, there are the animals, like Brer Rabbit from the U.S., Coyote of Mexico, and the mythical transformer-tricksters found so richly in Native American tradition.

In this book, you will meet both famous Asian tricksters and ordinary characters who played a good trick. The tales have been picked to be told aloud, and each is accompanied by an introduction, telling hints, resources, and follow-up activities. Since students learn in different ways, through different modalities and multiple intelligences, the activities are varied. Feel free to adapt and change them so that every learner is reached and challenged.

These trickster tales can be used to build skills in and enliven social studies, language arts, or library classes. Some teachers/librarians might want to use this book to start a storytelling unit, while others may wish to pursue the trickster theme as a separate unit. No matter what your interest, consider the following an introduction to tricksters, then find further ideas to develop storytelling in the next sections.

Getting Ready to Tell Trickster Tales

Encourage students to think about tricksters by telling them a trickster tale from this book or from your own background. Next, ask students for their favorite tricksters from stories around the world and from the media. List and discuss the characters, sharing a few favorite tricks.

Since most students like talking about themselves, ask as well for real tricks they played or had played on them. Such family tricks often involve food (pepper in soda to discourage a soda thief), clothing (tying someone's shoelaces together), camp (shortsheeting the bed), traps (water set up to fall when the door opens), school (ringing a bell at the wrong time), and much more.

If you'd like to involve parents at this point, you could ask each student to write a letter home, asking for more trick tales from the family's history.

Students can share such tricks in class discussions or in small groups. If you wish, individual pictures or collages of familiar tricks can be made. Or, the class can create a family trickster mural. Each student should draw at least one true trick on a small paper square, then all squares can be pasted on a large paper. Tricks can be scattered around the mural, or organized by type of trick, setting, victim, etc.

Once you've become familiar with tricks of all types, introduce your class to a few of the characters in this book. Then go on to use the guide together in the best way possible: reading the tales, telling them all or telling a few, exploring in depth, or just enjoying a good laugh.

Storytelling Basics for Teachers and Librarians

Why Tell Tales?

Why tell stories in an age of computers? Because the words of the storyteller reach across cultures, for stories speak to the heart first. Storytelling is the world's oldest teaching tool, and one which belongs in many settings. It will help students increase sensitivity to other cultures, times, and literature; develop aural comprehension and expressive oral skills; grow in self-confidence and self-knowledge; refine skills of editing, concentration, and so much more.

Getting Set to Tell

To encourage storytelling in your classroom or library, set the mood with the following ideas.

1. If possible, make a setting for storytelling: an informal space where students can gather on the floor or the ground close to a teller. Arrange to have the lights dimmed or curtains pulled when storytelling begins, to create a relaxed listening atmosphere.
2. Start a small storytelling resource center in the corner of your class or library with:
   - relevant books (handmade and published)
   - tapes of tellable tales
   - a story file with handouts of stories
   - a wall list of the stories told in your setting
   - a world story map marked with origins of these tales
   - tape recorders
   - simple musical instruments, puppets, and props
   - recycled and new materials to use for props: cardboard and paper, cloth bits, bamboo, colors, etc.
3. To stimulate the best student storytelling, try to tell many tales yourself and invite others to tell. Possible guest tellers include fellow librarians or teachers, parents and grandparents, travelers, or exchange students.

Finding the Right Tools

Storytelling tools range from imagination to the use of fingers and sound. As a teller (and guide of student tellers), you must use tools that are comfortable for you, that will appeal to your listeners, and that work with the various stories you tell. Different stories often call for different techniques, and everyone brings various abilities to the role of a storyteller. Try the following exercises and ideas to polish your skills along with those of your students.

Observation and Imagination

Use storytelling journals, or add a storytelling element to class journals. Write about characters and settings observed, names discovered, interesting sounds and stories heard, and ideas for plots, descriptions, and images that reach various senses.

Concentration and Visualization

- Picture the home(s) you grew up in, with as much detail as possible.
- Remember some of your happiest times, saddest times, times of anger or fright, etc.
- Read a newspaper article about an event, and draw a vivid sketch of it.

Breathing

- Take deep, slow breaths. Then try breathing in and out quickly as if panting. Use very little shoulder and chest movement. Instead, think of developing deeper, fuller breath support below.

Voice Work

- Stretch, yawn, shake, chew, laugh... such actions can help loosen up the muscles necessary for the best voice production.
- Sing simple melodies (e.g., lullabies or children's chants/songs) to use in some stories.
- Treat your voice as an instrument. Read a newspaper sentence in different ways, varying pitch, volume, texture, feeling, and rhythm.
- Talk in a monster's voice, give a king's command, or growl a lion's "***no!***"

Language

- Develop imagery through the use of poetry and traditional riddles.
- Remember repetition: try repeating words, phrases, and lists at various speeds to loosen the tongue.
- Consider the difference between words read and spoken. Choose words for their sounds: *awkward* is *awkward* to say, *rage* flows better than *anger*, and *shining* sounds different than *glittering*.

Gestures

- Practice miming a simple daily act: brushing your teeth, washing your face, eating soup. Try it at different speeds, with varying moods.
- Find someone who signs, in real life or on video, and learn some sign language to add to stories.

And the Rest

The list of storytelling tools could go on and on. Don't forget these other important tools for young tellers: a sensitivity to your audience and to story; eye contact; improvisation and collaboration; music and props; audience participation; enthusiasm and warmth.

Choosing Stories

In this book, you and your students will find a varied selection of trickster tales. The range of tales will assure that students with different strengths can find the story best suited for them. Urge students to choose a story that appeals to them. It is much easier to learn and shape a story that you like.

After you tell these trickster tales, encourage students to find other tales to share. As they search, remind them of these basic characteristics of tellable tales:

- limited and clearly drawn characters
- a plot that moves steadily on
- pleasing language
- possibilities for sound effects, music, or props
- vivid images
- elements of suspense, humor, drama, surprise, or pathos.

Learning Tales

These trickster tales are quite easy to remember since they have been shaped and edited. In the student how-to section, a variety of ways to learn a story are mentioned. Try to help students identify their own best learning styles and use their own strengths to learn a tale. Stories can be learned by:

- hearing the tale several times
- repeating it out loud (while alone or with friends)
- taping it
- mapping it
- drawing pictures of it
- acting it out
- outlining the plot.

Remind students that the story will change a little as it is learned, for that is the beauty of the oral tradition. Discourage memorizing, and encourage visualization. Memorized texts can sound quite stiff and may be suddenly forgotten when a teller feels nervous.

Shaping Tales

Once you know the basic plot, it is time to polish it, to make it suit your audience and your skills. Each story will demand different tools and decisions.

Gestures

Consider small or large gestures that might show a character: an old man stroking his beard, or a bird's light jump. Or add a gesture to show part of the setting: your hand sculpting the shape of a mountain.

Use gestures with care. They should not overwhelm the story, but enrich it. Be especially careful that you don't let nervous, ineffective gestures get in the way. Watch students, and try to stop such gestures before they are practiced into the tale.

When you tell these stories from Asia, make sure that a gesture is not offensive, e.g., when calling to people in Southeast Asia, the hand beckons with palm down (beckoning with palm up, as is done in some other places, would be used only with animals), and touching the head is considered impolite in much of Asia.

Language

Add just enough imagery to your stories, but don't overburden it. If desired, you or your students may add a few cultural details of plants, clothes, housing, or a rich description to these tales, but make sure the story still moves along.

Experiment with dialogue, let it lead the story on at times, allowing characters to come alive. Feel free to add or remove dialogue from the tales in this book. Some students feel more comfortable simply using a storytelling-narrator voice, with little dialogue. Others, who enjoy a bit of drama, may like to add distinctive character voices.

Encourage bilingual students to use pieces of their first language in the telling. They can most easily add such language in beginnings or endings, in the speech of certain characters, in the sounds of words and effects, in the names of characters or in the settings.

Silence and Pause

Beginning tellers, in their nervous haste to finish the story, often have trouble with these tools. Try a pause to build suspense or to underline a fine image: "he walked over to the closed door. Slowly, he opened it and saw" (pause....). You can also use a pause to strengthen a gesture: posing with a sword held high.

Rhythm and Repetition

Every tale has a rhythm; often, different parts of the story have different rhythms. These trickster tales are quite short and not so varied, but you may find places to speed up the tale or to slow it down for effect.

Look for scenes where a faster telling might add interest: a fight scene, a chase scene, a scene of children playing. Check for scenes where the story's rhythm should be slower: for a time of sickness, a scene with suspense, a frightening part of the tale.

Repetition is built into some of these trickster tales. If your students are telling these tales to younger students, they might be able to add more repetition—of a word, a phrase, a gesture. Younger listeners especially enjoy such word play.

Timing is another difficult tool to use, but a fine one. Listen to other tellers, speakers, and comedians, and watch how they use timing. Note when they hesitate before a punch line, pause to create tension, or show a fast-paced dialogue.

Sound Effects and Words

These marvelous tools will not be wanted in every story, but they are great fun to add. Students often come up with wonderful sound effects. Learning and using actual onomatopoeia from a culture is a fine challenge. The Japanese language is particularly full of such words, as you can see in the Japanese tales included here.

Audience Participation

As you and your students shape these tales, especially for young audiences, plan for the audience to sing or clap along, or to react to a signal you give. Students might feel reluctant to add audience participation, but as they gain storytelling confidence, encourage them to consider this option.

Music and Improvisation

In these trickster tales, there are not so many chances to add these tools. But you might still be able to use a small piece of a melody to begin or end a tale. Perhaps you could even add a percussion instrument to a telling.

Trying to add improvisation is much more difficult for most tellers, although it can work even in these trickster tales. Practice the art of story improvisation little by little, perhaps adding side comments to parts of a story: a remark about a related current event, or a relevant proverb, etc. If it works well, add some more; if not, don't worry—not everyone needs to improvise.

Putting It All Together with Props

Before you decide which tools will best suit and shape a story, look at the ideas for props, below. Props are not needed or wanted for every tale or every setting, but when they are used comfortably, with the right audience and story, they work well. Students often enjoy the security a prop gives them, so help them consider the following suggestions. If a story would be well-told with a prop, add the prop as you add your other tools. Then, after you've shaped your tale well, get ready to practice!

Asian storytelling props are varied: made of wood, bamboo, cloth, or paper. Visual storytelling props, from scrolls to cards, are the most popular types, and have been used for over two thousand years in busy Asian marketplaces, temples, festivals, and elsewhere. Try some in your class...

Kamishibai

Sets of pictures, first used in India to tell tales, turned up in early twentieth-century Japan as kamishibai (paper theater) sets of hand-painted cards. A roving kamishibai storyteller carried these sequenced story cards on his bicycle, seeking listeners and sales of food snacks. Today, published and handmade sets are often used by teachers and librarians in Japan, and recently also in Vietnam, Korea, and Singapore.

It is quite simple for tellers of all ages to make kamishibai sets. Instructions are included in Chapter 25, since that story is a fine one for kamishibai.

Scrolls

Handpainted scrolls, horizontal or vertical, are used in various parts of Asia to tell tales. Long sheets of light-colored paper can be used to make an easy version for the classroom; students can work in groups or partners to make them. Large-scale scenes, characters, and objects from the story can be drawn and painted on, or colorful paper cutouts can be pasted on. Then the tellers tell the tale while the sheet is placed behind them. To increase the drama, tellers can illuminate scenes with a candle or flashlight.

Hmong Story Cloths

The Hmong people, in Thai refugee camps and abroad, combine their stories and sewing skills into the creation of story cloths. These vibrant cloths share a story's images—characters, setting details, actions, even words—through bright embroidery often bordered with lively designs. To make a simple adaptation, take a large piece of dark paper, then paste on various large story objects cut from colored or tissue paper.

Folk Toys and Puppets

If you or your students have folk toys, crafts, or other objects from a story's culture, they can be woven into the telling at times. They also can be shown first to introduce a culture or story.

Designing original props is fun, using paper, cardboard, cloth bits, foam scraps, plastic bottles, wire, etc. Puppets can be made from various materials, in various sizes.

Practicing the Tale

Practice the finished story, with or without a prop, a number of times. Use a tape recorder, if possible, or tell it to an honest friend for feedback. When students rehearse, have them work with partners and in small groups, giving each other gentle, helpful critiques. Remember that storytelling is a talent—some of your students will be naturals, others won't, but everyone can improve. If students use a prop, allow time for students to practice the mechanics of its use, so that when they tell a tale, the prop doesn't distract them.

Use the questions below as a review checklist to help feedback (simplifying them if necessary), as you encourage individual strengths and differences.

- Is the teller relaxed? Does she show warmth and sensitivity to the audience? Is eye contact used effectively?
- Is the story plot clear? Does the teller know the tale and tell it without hesitation?

- How is the opening? Is the story about the right length?
- How is the voice used? Is it loud and clear enough to be heard? Does it share feelings at times? Does it vary in volume, texture, pitch, and inflection?
- Does the teller use character voices? If she does, are they easy to follow and not mixed up? Is dialogue used well and in the right amount?
- Is there descriptive language? Are there enough (but not too many) details to give listeners vivid word pictures?
- Is repetition used—in gesture, phrase, word, and sound? Could any be added?
- If sound effects or sound words are used, do they work well? If not, would some sounds enrich the telling?
- Would a pause add to the telling? Are gestures and expressions—of face, hands, and body—used? Do they add to the story? Are there any distracting gestures, nervous habits, or needless filler words?
- How is the timing and the rhythm of the story? Could the teller use varied story rhythms for different scenes and characters?
- Is there any active audience participation? If not, would a bit be welcome?
- If props are used, do they help the story, or get in the way?
- Is music used? Does it reflect the story's mood? Is it effective or distracting?

Telling to an Audience

Once the story is polished and ready, it needs to be told and retold, to be molded in front of live listeners. Make your storytelling a special time. Check that the setting is as conducive to listening as possible, with relaxed lighting, the audience seated close to the teller, and a quiet atmosphere. Take a few deep breaths (and suggest the same to your student tellers); then relax and enjoy it.

Helping Students Tell Tales

If you are guiding young storytellers, try to find various places for them to share stories besides your class or library: other classes and libraries, local day care agencies, senior centers, community centers. Encourage appropriate audience behavior before any tellers begin; you can remind younger listeners that storytelling takes work, that tellers are not TV sets (they're better!) and thus they need concentration. Challenge them to make many pictures in their minds as they listen, and ask them to hold any questions or comments until the story is over, so that the flow of the story is not broken.

Storytelling Basics for Students

Sharing a good story can be a lot of fun. Storytelling is an art that has been used around the world for centuries. Although some people are just natural storytellers, everyone can tell a tale. You can tell stories while babysitting, around the campfire, on long car rides, at slumber parties, in the library. If you really get serious about storytelling and practice hard, you can earn money by telling tales at birthday parties; you might even make it your career. So start now, and see where the telling leads...

Choosing and Learning a Story

The first rule of good storytelling is to choose a story you really like. If the story appeals to you, it will be much easier to learn and more fun to tell. When you choose a tale, remember your own talents. If you like to sing, choose a story that could include a song. If you like to draw, choose a story that might be told with a picture. If you are dramatic, find a story with good characters that you can bring to life. If you have a good sense of humor, use a tale that lets you share that. The trickster tales that follow should appeal to a range of talents and interests. Some are a little longer and harder to learn; others are simple and ready to share.

Once you find a good story, think of the best way to remember it. People learn in many different ways, so use any or all of the following to help you recall your story.

Picture It

Try visualization. Think of the story as a video—see each scene in your mind. Draw the characters or scenes from the story.

Outline or Map It

Make a map of the story, including important details of the plot, characters, and setting. Or if you like to write, make a brief outline of the plot, with details you want to remember.

Sculpt and Act It

Use your whole body to create the setting of the story and then to act out the tale. Involving action can help you remember details, feelings, and more.

Repeat it

Hear or read the story several times, imagining each scene as you do. If you have a tape recorder, try taping it, then listening to it carefully. Say it to yourself over and over. Share the tale casually with a friend. Tell it to a friendly tree or pet.

Shaping the Basics

Once the story feels comfortable and you can remember the whole thing, try to add any special touches to it. To make stories come alive, storytellers use voices, gestures, language, sound effects and silence, music, props, audience participation, and more. Each story is different—and each teller is too. Some stories sound great with lots of sound effects, others are best told in a quiet voice. Try any of these ideas below to shape your story.

- Use your voice as a clear, powerful tool. Show feelings through your voice. See if special sound effects can be added to spark interest: animal sounds, a heart beating, a door opening, a monster's roar, etc. Try a character voice or two if you feel comfortable.
- Add language that paints pictures, that really captures a character or setting. Use words that appeal to all the different senses.
- Try a few gestures—facial expressions, a wave of the hand, your whole body leaning forward—whatever will help your audience to feel the story.
- See if you can add a pause to create suspense, to emphasize a detail, or to invite a laugh.
- Consider the repetition of a sound, a phrase, or a good description.
- Think about adding some music or a chant.
- Remember that some stories are told with props—puppets, story cards, folk toys, felt boards, and more. Try making or finding a prop if you wish, then practice with it so it doesn't distract you when you tell the story.

Practicing and Feedback

Once you've added the final touches to your story, practice it several times. Tell it to yourself, or practice with a tape recorder or a friend. After you've gone over it, try your story out with a small group. Listen to the stories of your classmates, too, and act as guides for each other. Give helpful feedback on the use of voice, plot, gesture, sound, etc. Use the little checklist of possibilities below to help you to be a good storytelling guide.

Storytelling Tools

_____ A clear expressive voice

_____ Gestures that help the story (no nervous gestures)

_____ Language and details to give word pictures

_____ Sound effects

_____ Silence or a pause once in a while

_____ Eye contact with the audience

_____ Repetition of a word, gesture, or phrase

_____ A good beginning and ending

_____ Dialogue and/or character voices

_____ Audience participation

_____ Use of props or music

Tips for Real Telling

Now, you're ready to tell tales to bigger groups and to new audiences, too. Enjoy yourself when telling, for you are giving a gift to the audience. Look confident when you start, so they can relax and enjoy your tale. As you tell, use eye contact; find friendly faces in the audience, and use them to give you confidence.

Getting up to tell a tale in front of a group is a challenge. Many people of all ages feel nervous. To calm your nerves before you begin, breathe deeply in and out, stretch, laugh, give yourself a pep talk, or close your eyes and picture the story.

If you make a mistake or two, just keep telling. The audience probably won't even know you made a mistake unless you make a big deal out of it. So, just relax, and have fun telling your tale!

Part 2

The Tales

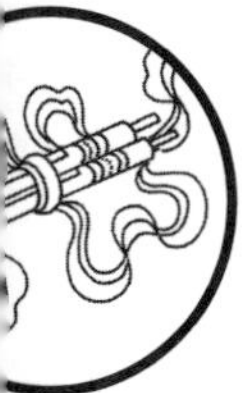

Chapter 1

Singapore

"The Missing Ticket" and "A Long Tale"

Singapore is an amazing country, where three cultural backgrounds—Chinese, Indian, and Malay—come together with past British links to form a twenty-first century identity as Singaporeans. Each group still relates to different roots and thus different people know various tricksters: Sang Kancil, Tenali Raman, foxes, and more. As for a new "Singapore" trickster, that identity is still evolving, although there are popular media characters as well as figures in jokes, like the foolish Ah Beng.

The Missing Ticket

One day, a navy diver got on the train in Singapore without money for a ticket. While he sat wondering what to do, he heard two Singapore soldiers talking, and he soon discovered that they had only one ticket between them.

"But what happens when the conductor comes?" asked the diver.

"We both squeeze into the bathroom, then push the one ticket under the door when he knocks," said one soldier. "He clips and returns it. We've done this many times, it always works."

Soon after that, the three men saw the conductor in the next car. Casually, the two soldiers went into the bathroom. A little while later, they heard a knock on the door and a voice called, "Ticket, please."

At once, one soldier slid the ticket under the door. The soldiers waited confidently for the clipped ticket to be returned. But the ticket never came back. With a grin, the diver quickly picked it up. Then he found a seat far away from the tricked and ticketless soldiers.

Telling Tips for "The Missing Ticket"

Jokes can be extremely difficult to tell. Timing is all-important. Make sure you pause before the punchline. You can add a little bit of characterization if you'd like, but don't go overboard—a joke is not a three act play.

A Long Tale

There was once an old monk who lived on top of the mountain with his disciples. One day, one monk asked for a story. All the little monks were sitting comfortably and getting ready to listen. So the old monk said,

There was once an old monk who lived on top of the mountain with his disciples. One day, one monk asked for a story. All the little monks were sitting comfortably and getting ready to listen. So the old monk said,

There was once an old monk who lived on top of the mountain with his disciples. One day, one monk asked for a story. All the little monks were sitting comfortably and getting ready to listen. So the old monk said,

There was once an old monk...

Telling Tips for "A Long Tale"

A good endless tale like this one should make listeners yell, **"Stop!"** It should be delivered in a very simple way, so that the cumulative effect of the words builds up. Don't pause too much as you tell, just keep repeating yourself over and over and over until your listeners realize the trick you've played on them.

Since this endless tale has few words, you could also try telling it in sign language. Find a book or video with sign language, or better still, a friend who knows it. Find signs for the important words in the story. If you get stuck, make up a sign, or use mime. Don't worry about signing each word, just the basics will do. As a beginner, you can use poetic license. Practice telling the story smoothly just in signs, then add your voice.

Activities

1. Jokes can also share tricks. Collect some jokes from friends, family, and joke books. Then put together some of the best jokes, with tricks and without, into a class joke book. Maybe you could even print and sell it.
2. Endless tales are a kind of verbal wordplay trick. They are also fun to create. But they are not easy to make, since the ending has to lead so perfectly around to the beginning. Find examples, and then try to make your own in partners. You can illustrate them in a fun way by drawing the story or printing the words on a long strip of paper, then fastening the ends together to make one long loop—an endless tale in paper.

Resources

Charlip, Remy. 1997. *Arm in Arm.* Tricycle Press. A delightful collection of wordplays, jokes, and endless tales.

Feinberg, Leonard, ed. 1971. *Asian Laughter.* Weatherhill. A fine collection of Asian jokes and other humor, best as a teacher resource.

Marsh, Valerie. 1995. *Beyond Words: Great Stories for Hand and Voice.* Alleyside Press. A collection of twenty more tales to tell with sign language.

Korea

"A Fine Moon"

In Korean folklore, the magistrate or scholar can be the butt of tricks and jokes. In reality, the magistrate wielded power in traditional Korea, and so the stories of tricks played against him were a kind of release in a strict, hierarchical society. A favorite trick of the traditional Korean trickster/con man Kim Sondal concerns the time he sold a river to some greedy rich men.

A clever girl advising her father can be found in tales around the world. It is interesting that although there are many such stories of clever girls, it is rare to find many stories about one clever female (as we find for male tricksters). The stories seem, instead, to be about many different characters.

A Fine Moon

One day, a rich Korean magistrate moved to a new city for work. That night in his home, he stared out at the lovely full moon above a nearby pond. But two weeks later, when he looked out, the moon was almost gone. There was only a sliver left for him to see. He called at once for his servant.

"That beautiful old moon is dying. There is almost nothing left of it. Therefore you must buy me another full moon at once, for a good price," he demanded. "Or you will lose your job." Much upset, the servant went home, where his young daughter saw his sad face.

"Father, why is your face like the monsoon clouds?" she asked.

"I must buy a full moon for our foolish magistrate or lose my job. How can I ever buy something in the sky?" he cried.

"I can help, father," she said with a smile, and told him what to do. The next day, he walked proudly up to the magistrate.

"Sir, I have ordered a lovely moon," he said with a bow. "It will come soon. But you must keep your window closed until it arrives. Please do not look out, for we will be busy arranging the moon and must not be disturbed." The silly magistrate happily agreed.

After two weeks, when the real moon had changed its shape and was again full, the servant came in one evening.

"You are very fortunate, sir," he said as he bowed. "We have bought a superior moon. At last we have finished placing it over the pond.

Your new moon indeed looks quite wonderful. Allow me to open the window so that you may enjoy it."

With a flourish, the servant opened the window and the magistrate eagerly stepped up to it, then gazed out at a lovely full moon.

"You have bought a fine moon, and you shall be well rewarded," said the magistrate, smiling with pleasure. Then he sighed in awe, stroked his beard and said, "Beautiful, isn't it?"

Telling Tips for "A Fine Moon"

This is a short tale which doesn't need many actions or voices. If you like, you can show how worried the servant is and how wise the daughter seems. And at the end, you can make the magistrate appear even more foolish, if you exaggerate a bit to show how pleased he is at his new moon (by a nice, big sigh, or a grand, large wave of the hand, etc.). For fun, if you feel like making a prop, you can make a nice, bright full moon and hold it up for all to admire at the end of the tale.

Activities

1. Drawing a picture after hearing a tale is a fun way to remember the story. Since this is about the moon, try drawing part of the tale on a moon-shaped paper. To be really fancy, you could make a window, with paper shutters opening to show the moon underneath. The story could be drawn either on the shutters or on the moon.
2. It can be quite simple to fool such silly people. Make this magistrate into a foolish twentieth-century politician in the U.S. or elsewhere, then write a trick to play on him/her. Or draw a political cartoon to show the trick.
3. This girl, like many wise girls in folklore, advises her father quite often. Create a letter she might write to a far-off cousin, telling about some of the other times she helped her father or family with advice, and sharing her feelings about these experiences.

Resources

Phelps, Ethel. *The Maid of the North.* Holt, Rinehart, and Winston, 1981. A classic source of tales about strong girls.

Sherman, Josepha. *Rachel the Clever and Other Jewish Folktales.* August House, 1993. A look at another clever girl from the Jewish tradition.

Spagnoli, Cathy. *Asian Tales and Tellers.* August House, 1998. This collection of Asian tales includes the story of Kim Sondal's river sale.

Thailand

"Jump In"

Thanonchai
pronounced
TAHN-ON-CHIE

Sri Thanonchai seems to be related to A-Chey and Sieng Mieng of Southeast Asia. Some of the same tricks are told of all three. He has not traveled quite as far as A-Chey (who went to China), although some of his tricks were played against characters from other countries, too (like the time he fooled a Burmese during a fight between two buffaloes).

The story of Sri Thanonchai has been shared not only by storytelling, but in temple murals, comic books, movies, and novels. Anecdotes about the trickster were shared to demonstrate how sharp wit can help one survive, although many of his tricks are best for adult listeners. He tricked a range of people in authority, from his parents to his king. And although he grew less successful in older age, he still managed, while on his deathbed, to trick the king one last time.

Jump In

Once in Thailand, there lived Sri Thanonchai, a man who played many tricks very well. The king heard of him and decided to test him. So one morning, the king dressed in simple clothes and rode on his royal elephant to the village where Sri Thanonchai lived. He soon found Sri Thanonchai relaxing in front of his house, next to the river.

"That's a fine elephant," said Sri Thanonchai.

"Yes," replied the disguised ruler. "It belongs to the king. I work at the palace."

"Ah," said Sri Thanonchai. "You must be quite clever to work there."

"Yes," agreed the king. "I am almost as smart as the king himself."

"Oh no," said Sri Thanonchai. "No one is that clever. The king is a very, very wise man."

"Well, some people say you are as clever as the king."

"Never," said Sri Thanonchai.

"You may be," said the king. "So I have come to test you, to see if you are as tricky as people say."

"What kind of test do you mean?" asked the trickster.

"Well, let us see if you can make me jump into the river," suggested the king.

"That's too hard," said Sri Thanonchai rather lazily. "I could never make you jump into the river. However, if you were already in the river, I bet I could make you come out!"

"I doubt it," said the king. He suddenly jumped into the river, then shouted, "Just try to get me out. I don't think you can."

"But I don't have to make you come out," said the trickster with a smile. "You told me to make you jump in. I just did. You can stay in the water as long as you wish, I don't care. I already proved myself more clever than you."

The king was at first very annoyed. But then he laughed and climbed out of the river. "You win," he said. "I bow to your clever mind." Then the very wet king returned to his palace, while Sri Thanonchai took a nap with a lazy smile on his face!

Telling Tips for "Jump In"

This is a simple tale, with only two characters. Use your expressions to show how lazy and simple Sri Thanonchai appears. Think about how a king would sound; then imagine him in disguise and give the right tone to his voice.

Activities

1. The king comes to Sri Thanonchai in this tale. Many tricksters around the world seem to play tricks on kings, sometimes just fooling them as in this one, sometimes teaching them a lesson. Imagine you had a chance to play a trick on the governor of your state. What kind of trick would you play? Would you play one to teach him how to be a better governor, or just to trick him? Describe, draw, or act out your trick.
2. Think of other ways that Sri Thanonchai could trick the king into entering the river. Make a cluster map of possibilities—with the problem in a center circle, and possible ideas each sketched or written in different circles coming off center.

Resources

Edmonds, I. G. 1966. *Trickster Tales.* Lippincott. This fine older collection includes several tales of tricksters tricking rulers.

Leichman, Seymour. 1968. *The Boy Who Could Sing Pictures.* Doubleday. Although this boy is not a traditional trickster, he teaches the king in this lovely story (which is a fine one to tell, as well).

Laos

"On the Farm"

The dog is not a traditional trickster in Laos. The most famous trickster there is the human Sieng Mieng, featured elsewhere. But the tale of the tricky dog is a nice example of a "how and why" tale caused by a trick. The tale might also spark discussion about the traits of a dog in various stories: from the tales where dogs rescue humans to those where he seems to be a lazy rascal. Although dogs are not often tricksters, students might like to read about another tricky dog in Reneaux's book below.

On the Farm

Once in Laos, there was a hardworking pig. He lived on a farm with a farmer, his wife, and their dog. One sunny day, the man turned to his wife.

"I am going to work in the field now," he said. "The dog and the pig will come with me." Then the three went to work. They passed by coconut trees and bamboo leaves, and soon reached the field. The farmer and the pig worked and worked. But the dog just slept.

The wife stayed home and cooked sticky rice with fish. Then she stepped down from the house to the ground and set off to get her husband and the animals.

"Come and eat," she called.

"Let's go," said the husband to the animals. "It's time to eat."

"Go ahead, I'm coming soon," yawned the dog. After they left, the dog jumped up, then ran and ran all around the field. Next he went home and joined the others.

Before she served the food, the wife asked, "Who worked the hardest today?"

"I worked hard," said the husband, "and so did the pig. But that dog didn't do anything. He just slept under the tree."

"You're wrong," said the dog. "I worked the hardest of all. If you don't believe me, go to the field and see for yourself."

"Let's go and take a look," said the wife. "Then I will know who is telling the truth."

So the woman, the man, the dog, and the pig went to the field. There they saw the dog's footprints. The footprints were everywhere, covering the field, like the eyes of a peacock's feathers. The man, the woman, and the pig just stared at the fields, while the dog wagged his tail proudly. Then they all returned home.

"That dog certainly did work hard," said the wife. "I saw all those footprints." She smiled at the dog and gave him a huge dish of the best food. Then she gave just a little hard rice to the pig.

"***Noooo, noooo,***" stamped the pig. "That dog is lying. If you're going to treat him so nicely, then I'm leaving." Then the poor pig ran away to the forest and stayed there, very mad, from that day on.

The lazy dog ate his food very happily, then curled up to sleep. He lived the same lazy life every day, quite content. But the couple soon grew sad, for the pig never came back. And the lazy dog never changed. So they had no help for the fieldwork, and lived most unhappily ever after.

Telling Tips for "On the Farm"

You might want to include some contrasting character voices for the pig and the dog. When you describe the dog running around the field, your hands could show the pattern of tracks. Since this story has several settings and an interesting last scene with footprints, this would be a nice story to tell with kamishibai cards (see Chapter 25 for instructions).

Activities

1. Although short, this story raises some interesting questions for a class discussion:

   Was the ending fair?

   What is the moral of this story? Do you agree with it?

   Why do you think the dog was mean to the pig?

   Could the ending be changed to be fair, yet still funny?

2. Poor pig has to leave and go to the forest. She is not very happy there. Write the letters she might write, if she could, to the couple and to the dog.

Resources

Hausman, Gerald. *The Mythology of Dogs.* St. Martin's Press, 1997. Rich source of stories and anecdotes about the dog, from various cultures.

Reneaux, J. J. *Why Alligator Hates Dog.* August House, 1995. In the Louisiana bayous, Dog tricks Alligator, king of the swamps.

Chapter 5

Laos

"Your Thoughts"

Sieng Mieng (or Xieng Mieng) of Laos is usually portrayed as a villager who manages to trick and fool the king and others in power. He seems quite similar to Sri Thanonchai of Thailand and A-Chey of Cambodia, although his career is not as varied as A-Chey's, and he doesn't seem to have traveled as far from his home. But he, too, is well-liked and his tricks widely enjoyed. He sometimes plays a trick by responding too literally to an order; at other times he uses simplicity to teach a lesson.

Your Thoughts

In long-ago Laos, Sieng Mieng often needed money for his big family. So one day, when the food supply was running especially low, he turned to his wives.

"Bring me some empty bags. And be ready to cook a feast tonight," he said. Then he marched to the king's palace.

All of the king's ministers were meeting, getting ready to advise the king. Sieng Mieng walked up and stood waiting to speak. Finally, one minister turned and said, "We are busy now, come back later."

"Sir," said Sieng Mieng. "I came to offer my services. I can do something very strange. I can see the future. And I can read your minds. I can tell what each of you is thinking right now."

"That's impossible," said the official. "You are not a fortune-teller, you are a mischief maker!"

"I am just a plain man," replied Sieng Mieng, "except for my unusual talent."

"This is another of your tricks," said the official. "But this time you will be caught. At last you will be punished for your lies. Let us go before the king now, and you tell him our thoughts."

"Certainly," agreed Sieng Mieng. "And if I can say what you are thinking, then my bags must be filled with gold. If I cannot, then you must punish me."

All the officials agreed. They walked together to the throne room and asked for permission to speak to the king. When the king was ready, the ministers told him of Sieng Mieng's challenge.

"All right, Sieng Mieng," said the king. "I shall be the judge. Tell me exactly what each of my ministers is thinking right now."

Sieng Mieng looked slowly at each of the ministers, then smiled at the king.

"Your highness," he said with a bow. "Each of them is thinking what a wonderful, wise king you are."

The ministers suddenly looked very confused. If they disagreed with Sieng Mieng, the king would be angry. If they agreed, then Sieng Mieng would win. For a moment, no one spoke.

"Come, now," said the king, growing annoyed and a little suspicious. "Is this true or not?"

"Yyess," said the chief minister slowly. "That is correct, sir. We were all thinking indeed what a fine king you are."

The king smiled, well pleased. He ordered that Sieng Mieng's bags be filled with gold. So, while the ministers fumed in frustration, Sieng Mieng left with the gold and a grin.

Telling Tips for "Your Thoughts"

This is a rather short, straightforward tale which doesn't need too much embroidery. The action is direct and simple, and the telling should be as well. You can show the king's royal manner if you wish, and perhaps show the expressions of one or two ministers by a turn of your head. And, to add a little suspense about Sieng Mieng's mind reading, you could pause right before he tells the king what everyone is thinking.

Activities

1. Make a before-and-after cartoon of the story. In the first frame, put the court scene. Draw bubbles for the real thoughts of each minister, and the bubble of Sieng Mieng's winning remark. In the second scene, draw Sieng Mieng leaving with the gold and the ministers watching. Draw bubbles for the thoughts of everyone at that time. (Try to give different personalities to the ministers: some amused, some angry, some jealous, etc.)
2. Imagine Sieng Mieng in front of the U.S. President and the Cabinet, making the same bet. What witty reply could he give to win? How would he describe his trick later on the Oprah Winfrey show?

Resources

Hodge, Anthony. *Cartooning.* Gloucester Press, 1992. A how-to book to help beginning cartooners.

Kaignavongsa, Xay and Hugh Fincher. *Legends Of The Lao.* Geodata System, 1993. A nice range of stories collected in Laos, with a good section on Sieng Mieng.

Tibet

"Agu Tompa Borrows a Pot"

Agu
pronounced
AH-GOO

Agu or Uncle Tompa is a rascal well loved among Tibetans. Even though his exploits are often risqué, and not all can be shared in an elementary or middle school, he remains a fun-loving, likable character. He enjoys life and never gives respect simply because someone is a monk or a rich man. He fools those in a nunnery as happily as he fools those in a mansion.

Tibetans in this century have suffered greatly; they have lost their freedom, their homes, and their loved ones. Both Tibetans in Tibet and Tibetan refugees abroad enjoy these tales, for Agu Tompa is an important symbol. As a symbol of someone who, through his tricks, often fights social injustice or abuse of power, Agu Tompa imparts to us the rich Tibetan sense of humor and love of life, and inspires listeners to use wit and confidence as they move through an often difficult life.

Agu Tompa Borrows a Pot

Once in Tibet, there lived a man named Agu Tompa. He was a clever man who loved to trick others, especially the rich and mighty. One day he went to a very stingy rich man and asked to borrow a large copper pot. Agu Tompa promised to return it quickly and safely, so at last the rich man agreed.

Several days later, Agu Tompa returned to the rich man's house. He carried a cloth-covered object.

"Congratulations," he said to the rich man.

"Why?" asked the miser.

"Because your pot has given birth. It had a beautiful little son," said the trickster.

"You fool," said the rich man. "How can a pot have a child?"

"I don't know how it was done," replied Agu Tompa. "But I can show you the baby." And he took the cloth off of a lovely little copper pot, which was shaped just like the big one.

"Here, take it. Since the mother belongs to you, the son does as well," said Agu Tompa. Now the rich man knew that a pot could not give birth. But since he was offered a free pot, he happily took it.

"Thank you," he said, gazing at the pot proudly. "He certainly does look like his mother, doesn't he? Now please take good care of the mother; then she may have more children."

Agu Tompa promised to do so and soon left. After a few days, however, he again came to the rich man. This time, his face was very, very sad.

"I have terrible news," he cried with a sob. "Your pot has died."

"***Nonsense***," roared the rich man. "How can a pot die?"

"If a pot can give birth, then a pot can die," replied Agu Tompa calmly. The rich man was furious. But what could he say? He had already accepted the little pot. After a moment he shouted, "Well then if she has died, at least give me her body to bury."

"I am so sorry, but I already cremated her," replied the trickster.

"Where?" asked the miser, growing more and more furious.

"At the blacksmith's," said Agu Tompa, hiding a smile.

"You're a cheat!" cried the man. "You stole my big pot. Give it back to me."

"You're a cheat," said Agu Tompa. "You stole my little pot. Give it back to me."

The two kept shouting and fighting until neighbors began to gather. Finally, the rich man grew embarrassed and gave up. He slammed the door shut and went into his home. Agu Tompa turned around and went home to enjoy his nice, big copper pot.

Telling Tips for "Agu Tompa Borrows a Pot"

Since there are only two characters in this tale, it is quite easy to portray them in two distinct ways. Agu Tompa is probably the more dramatic of the two—just like any good con man, he can be very convincing whether showing sadness or joy. The miser is greedy for money, perhaps a bit grasping in his manners. Show his inner struggle when he gets the baby pot: he knows that this "birth" cannot be true, but he selfishly wants to get something for nothing. His anger at the final trick is increased when he realizes how well he's been fooled.

Activities

1. Agu Tompa is a delightful rogue. His trick here is a sly one. What would happen if the miser went to a judge and demanded justice? Write the court's decision.

2. Making exact models, big and small, just like the copper pot and its child, can be a fun project. At home, use available materials to make something in two sizes: either draw two exact copies large and small (***Do not*** use a copy machine!) or make them from folded paper, clay, cardboard, etc.

Resources

Dorje, Rinjing. *Tales of Uncle Tompa.* Station Hill Arts, 1997. A marvelous collection of Uncle Tompa stories.

Tibet Online *www.tibet.org*

Comprehensive site on Tibet, including culture, environment, resources, links, and more.

Chapter 7

China

"To Trick a Thief"

This tale features a popular character in many folktales: the clever old man. He is not so much the wise old man or sage, to whom people go for guidance, but the "street-smart" older man who has learned how to get by with his wits. The rich culture of China has produced learned scholars, hermit poets, brave bandits, and this type of clever man.

An interesting note here concerns the age of tricksters. When you examine the world's tricksters, most are portrayed in their prime. They play tricks usually as young or middle-aged men. These same tricksters must age, but we don't hear as much of their tricks in later years—perhaps they just calm down and get settled into marriages and home life. Due to this lack of elder tricksters, the following tale is fun to share.

To Trick A Thief

Once at an inn in long-ago China, an old man sat down. He soon started talking with some travelers. They turned out to be thieves, who boasted of their skills.

"Are you really so clever at stealing?" asked the old man. "Tell me exactly what you can do."

"Well, we can quickly dig through a wall," said one.

"And we can climb easily up on a roof," said another.

"We move quietly through a house while people still sleep," added the leader.

"Well, I may be a better thief than any of you," bragged the old man.

"Why... What can you do?" asked the leader.

"I can make a dog stop barking when I go up to a house. And I can make a door open without lifting my hand or waking up anyone."

The thieves were interested in these skills, since they could prove to be very useful.

"Please have dinner with us, kind sir," said the leader. "And then if you would be so kind, perhaps you could demonstrate your talent."

The old man happily agreed, for he was very hungry and also quite poor. He ate a fine meal with many delicacies, and when at last it was finished, he spoke.

"Now I shall show you my skills," he said. "We will go to the house of a poor family that now has a rare piece of jade." With greedy eyes, the thieves followed the old man. But they didn't know that he led them right to his own house.

"Wait here," he ordered, then left them at the edge of the woods. As he walked up to his house, a dog started to bark furiously. Then the thieves watched in amazement. For when the old man raised his hand slowly, the dog was suddenly silent.

Eagerly, the thieves kept watching. The old man went to the door. At once the door opened and he went inside.

"The man is very talented indeed," whispered the thieves to each other. Of course, they didn't know that the dog had smelled his master, and that the wife had opened the door for her husband.

Inside the house, the man picked up a worthless stone. He told his wife to cry, "thieves," when he stood on a nearby bridge. Then he ran out to the thieves, holding his hand tightly as if guarding a treasure.

"Quick, I have the jade," he cried. "Let us run before they find out!" The four men ran, and when they were on the bridge, the old man put out his hand to give them the jade. The leader stretched out his hand to take it. But just then, a loud shout, "***Thieves!***" was heard from the house.

"***Splash!***" The river cried as the old man suddenly dropped the stone, as if by accident. Quite frightened, the thieves ran swiftly away, never to return.

So, with a full stomach and a pleased grin, the man went home to share his tale with his wife.

Telling Tips for "To Trick a Thief"

Build up the character of the old man as skilled and confident. Add a dog's bark if you'd like and a grand wave of the hand to open the door. Use a loud whisper to show the old man talking to his wife. Make the final action of the "jade" falling into the river very obvious. You might slow down that scene slightly—hold out your hand, and then, at just the right moment, shout "***Thieves,***" and mime the jade falling. Add a good, loud splash with your voice if you wish. End with the frightened faces of the thieves and the clever smile of the old man.

Activities

1. Choose one of the younger tricksters in this book and make him age. Create one last trick that he/she would play before death (or that will be played after death, according to any last wishes or instructions).

2. Imagine that the old man lives today in the U.S. and tricks some high-tech thieves trying to break into a bank. As a class, brainstorm what kind of trick he might play using the latest technologies (even some not invented yet that students might dream up).

Resources

The Trickster Page
http://members.aol.com/pmichaels/glorantha/foolsparadise.html
A wonderful site on the trickster, old and young, with links to various cultures and time periods.

Burma

"A Fair Trade"

In older Burma (now called Myanmar), law students were given stories to debate—stories of both actual court cases and imaginary ones. Princess Learned-in-the-Law, the heroine of the fictional cases (many based on real events), is important as one of folklore's few female judges. In *Burmese Law Tales*, Burmese law scholar Maung Htin Aung writes that although Princess Learned-in-the-Law was a fictional character, "a woman 'headman,' or a woman arbitrator, or a queen meting out justice was common in Burmese society [due to]... the social and legal equality of Burmese women with Burmese men" (p. 22).

A number of the Princess's cases either had tricks in them or were solved with wit or a trick. Thus she joins the ranks of similar wise and often "tricky" judges such as Judge Bao of China, Judge Ooka of Japan, King Solomon, Judge Rabbit of Cambodia, and others.

A Fair Trade

A Burmese trader once went to a merchant friend and asked, "Will you please store these iron plowshares for me while I'm away?"

The merchant, who had greedy eyes and a lying heart, smiled and eagerly agreed. He led the trader to the storeroom and they left the plowshares safely there. After several days, however, the merchant secretly moved them to another one of his storerooms.

Months later, when the trader went to reclaim his tools, the merchant put on the saddest face.

"What a terrible shame," he moaned. "I am so, so sorry. Come see what has happened." And he led the trader to the storeroom where the plowshares had been. In their place, one could see only bits and pieces of some rats' nests.

"I did my best to guard them," said the merchant. "But the rats here are very strong and they have eaten your plowshares. Please accept my great apologies."

Although he knew that rats could never eat iron plowshares, the trader could not call the merchant a liar. So he left, with anger in his heart. At home, he planned his revenge.

The next week, the trader invited the merchant's son to go bathe in the river. He treated him kindly, but after several hours, he hid him in a friend's home. That evening, when his son had still not returned, the merchant went to the trader's house.

"Where is my son?" he cried.

"What a terrible shame," said the trader. "I am so, so sorry. Your son was playing happily by the river, when suddenly a hawk came and carried him away."

"That's nonsense," cried the merchant. "A bird cannot carry off a boy. Where is he? What have you done?"

"Dear friend," replied the trader. "If rats can eat iron plowshares, then a hawk can take your son."

The two argued for hours and hours. Then finally they took their case to Princess Learned-in-the-Law. She listened carefully to both sides and realized that the cheater had been cheated.

"You must somehow return the plowshares. And then your son will be returned to you," she ordered. "Then be friends again and live in harmony."

The two men left, and soon after, both men received what they wanted and renewed their friendship. And, to this day, the story's lesson is shared in a Burmese saying:

"The iron plowshares have been eaten by rats, and the child has been carried off by a hawk."

Telling Tips for "A Fair Trade"

Although there is little description of the Princess in her tales, a Burmese woman is expected to be modest and polite. Thus your voice can show the calm of Princess Learned-in-the-Law in contrast to the anger of the two men.

Sometimes when telling a tale, you must introduce a story detail so that everything is clear. Since the ending proverb is important, make sure listeners know that a plowshare is the cutting blade of a plow. And when you finish the tale, with the proverb, speak it slowly, so that the words will stay with your listeners.

Activities

1. **For Teachers** Princess Learned-in-the-Law is an unusual character. If she lived today, she might be as popular as TV's Judge Judy. Discuss some of the judges on television, then make your own class courtroom. Have small groups each prepare a case to solve—with defendant, plaintiff, and

problem—using the resources below. Invite each group to present their case, with students acting as defendant and plaintiff; then have the class debate a verdict.

2. **For Students** Since Princess Learned-in-the-Law is a fine role model, she deserves a postage stamp in her honor. Create one using her portrait, a general design, a symbol from her case, a proverb that she might use, or other details from Burma. Make the stamp big enough to see details, add the postal rate, and use colors and bold lines as needed.

Resources

Aung, Maung Htin. *Burmese Law Tales.* Oxford University Press, 1962.

Creeden, Sharon. *Fair is Fair: World Folktales of Justice.* August House, 1996..

Edmonds, I. G. *The Case of The Marble Monster.* Scholastic, 1973.

Renberg, Dalia. *King Solomon and the Bee.* HarperCollins, 1994.

Chapter 9

Thailand

"The Painting Contest"

This trick by the popular Thai trickster, Sri Thanonchai, is actually quite well known in Asia, also played by a scholar trickster in Vietnam and Sieng Mieng of Laos. In India, trickster Tenali Raman plays similar tricks by interpreting paintings.

Sri Thanonchai is also known for a number of rather risqué tricks that just can't be shared in school. And, unlike some tricksters of old, he has moved very nicely into the modern age. There are books published about his tricks today, including one on a jet-age Sri Thanonchai.

The Painting Contest

The king of Thailand had a painting contest one warm morning. People of many backgrounds came to show their skill. Papers were spread out, with ink and brushes ready to be used.

"This contest will be brief," said the king. "The royal gong will be struck only once. Your painting must be done as soon as the gong stops ringing. Whoever makes the best painting in that time will be declared the winner."

Although their faces remained calm, many people felt suddenly uneasy. It was impossible to paint a picture in so little time. Yet, they had to try. And so they stood, hands poised nervously over the papers. Only one man, the tricky Sri Thanonchai, looked confident, for he had a plan.

"***Donnnnnn***," sounded the gong. Its deep tones lasted several minutes, yet not long enough. Most of the men carefully picked up their brushes and wet them with ink. But just as their brushes moved close to their papers, the room grew silent. The gong was still. The contest was over and almost every paper was blank.

Sri Thanonchai's paper, though, was covered with a most unusual design. Five wavy lines danced over it, from top to bottom. For when he heard the drum, Sri Thanonchai quickly dipped his five fingers in the ink, and pulled them across the paper. Thus, while others struggled with fine brushes, Sri Thanonchai fingerpainted. And since he was the only one with a finished work, he was declared the winner.

"Now I wish to know the meaning of your painting," commanded the king.

"Your Honor," replied Sri Thanonchai with a bow. "It has many different and deep meanings. But I shall tell you the simplest meaning, so that everyone here may understand. It can be called, 'Five Worms Walking.'"

The king, pleased with the painting and the wit behind it, rewarded him well. Thus, in this way, Sri Thanonchai won a painting contest—using his brains instead of a brush.

Telling Tips for "The Painting Contest"

You don't have to dress up this simple tale, but you can show the slow movements of the other people as they prepare to paint. And you could swing something imaginary to hit the gong and make a good, long sound as you do. Then, in contrast to it, show how quickly Sri Thanonchai dips his fingers and paints.

Activities

1. Using your imagination, as Sri Thanonchai does, is very important. To stimulate creativity, try playing the scribble game in partners. Take a large piece of plain paper. Have one partner make a scribble—a short line of any type or design. Then the second partner must add to the scribble to turn it into a simple sketch or figure: a wavy scribble might turn into an ocean with a boat, a V-like scribble might be a rabbit's ear.
2. Tricksters often use their imagination. Explore the web sites below and try several of the creative activities mentioned e.g., mind mapping, visual thinking, lateral thinking puzzles, and more.

Resources

Creativity Web *www.ozemail.com.au/~caveman/Creative/index.html*

A wonderful site for all ages on creativity, with activities, articles, and resources

Enchanted Mind *www.enchantedmind.com*

Creatively designed site to help locate resources and materials on imagination and creativity.

New Horizons in Learning *www.newhorizons.org*

A rich site for educators and older students who wish to develop imagination, creativity, and work for the schools of tomorrow.

Chapter 10

Malaysia

"Sang Kancil and the Lion"

In Malaysia, people love to share tales of Sang Kancil. He is a tiny mousedeer, shaped like a deer, but under 10 cm. (3.937 inches) long. His exploits are known and shared in Indonesia, too. Sang Kancil often tricks large animals like a tiger or a lion. At times, he helps humans as well, as in "The Stolen Scents" (page 64). He lives freely in the jungle and is quite pleased with his life. The lush Malay jungle takes care of his needs and the other animals respect his wit and confidence. Students will recognize him as a folkloric cousin to Brer Rabbit, Coyote, Reynard the Fox, and other smaller, tricky animal characters. But he does seem to be unique—since he is the only mousedeer trickster in the world!

Sang Kancil *pronounced SAHNG KAHN-CHEEL*

Sang Kancil and the Lion

Once there lived a very powerful lion in a large Malay jungle. All of the other animals were scared of his roar. They declared him their king, hoping he would be kind. But he was a mean and frightening ruler. Every day, he attacked the small and weak. Every day, he ate some poor little animal.

Soon, the animals spent most of their time hiding from the king. Even the biggest animals ran away when he hungrily prowled. At last, the unhappy animals came together to plan.

"The lion is too strong and cruel," said the elephant. "We need a new king."

"But there is no one more powerful," a monkey chattered. "Who can take his place?"

"Perhaps we need someone smarter, not stronger," suggested a wise old tiger. "Maybe Sang Kancil will agree to be king."

The animals were pleased with that idea. Sang Kancil was the clever, tiny mousedeer who loved to play tricks and use his wit. A small bird was sent to beg him to be king, and he agreed at once.

But although there was now a new king, nothing really changed. The lion still killed and frightened just about everyone. Every day, some animal ran to the new king and complained.

At last Sang Kancil grew very sad. "The animals trusted me," he thought. "I must help them. I must get rid of the lion and make the jungle safe. Otherwise I will not be a good king."

He scratched his little ear and thought for some time. Then he smiled. He had a plan. Early the next morning, he bowed before the lion.

"Excuse me, great sir," he said. "But may I dare to ask you a question?"

"What is it, you little pest?" roared the lion. ***"Speak up or I'll eat you up!"***

"I just wondered," whispered Sang Kancil. "Since you are so big and strong, is there anything that you are scared of?"

"Me?" the lion cried. ***"Scared? Never! There is nothing that scares me. But what about you, you measly thing? You are so weak, you must be afraid of everything!"***

"No, sir," replied Sang Kancil. "I am only afraid of human beings."

"Human beings?" said the lion. "What are they?"

"Come and I will show you," said the mousedeer. Then he took the lion on a long trail that led to a village. After some time, they saw an old man walking and leaning on a cane.

"Is that a human being?" asked the lion.

"No," said Sang Kancil. "He is walking on three legs. Humans only have two." And so they walked on and on. At last, they came to a clearing where they saw three hunters.

"Those are humans," said the mousedeer. "Why not jump out to show them you are not afraid."

The lion crouched, then **jumped** at the men. Surprised, they shot their arrows at the lion, and disappeared. Moaning in pain, the lion realized he'd been shot, and fell down. Sang Kancil came and carefully pulled out an arrow.

"Thank you, friend," said the lion. "I almost died from those terrible human beings. They are indeed very fierce. I don't want to stay anywhere near them. I am going far away so that they can't hurt me again." Then the lion painfully dragged himself away, never to return. And Sang Kancil, with a pleased grin, ran back to share the good news with all his friends.

Telling Tips for "Sang Kancil and the Lion"

If you like to make character voices, this tale is for you. A good lion's roar would be very effective. And when he is wounded by the arrows, make his cry of pain heard. You can also surprise your audience when the lion jumps out at humans by raising your voice suddenly as he **jumps**! For a variety of moods or to make the tale a little longer, you can add an animal or two sadly telling Sang Kancil about their problems.

Decide on a way to portray the little mousedeer. Would you like to have him scratch his head while he thinks? Should he give his head a little shake? Well planned gestures can help identify a character. Think, too, about Sang Kancil's voice—it can be small because of his size, but it must still be heard.

Activities

1. This story takes place around the jungle, and could lend itself well to a map of animal homes, places of trouble with the lion, clearings where humans were spotted, etc. Take a large paper and some colors and create an aerial map to show these places and more.
2. Small animal tricksters all around the world have tricked large, powerful animals like lions, tigers, and elephants. In class, see if you can remember one or two such tricks, to compare with this one. Make a list of "Handy Tricks to Try if You are Weak and They are Strong!" Or, if you have access to a video camera, this theme would make a great, fun (and funny) topic for a short video.

Resources

Aardema, Verna. *Rabbit Makes a Monkey of Lion.* Dial, 1989. Another small trickster fools another lion.

Spagnoli, Cathy. *Kantjil and Tiger.* The Wright Group, 1995. This funny picture book shares three tricks Sang Kancil played on tiger.

Vietnam

"Why the Water Buffalo Can't Talk"

In Vietnam there are various tricksters. Because learning and scholarship were historically important, several of the tricksters, like Trang Quyenh, were learned men who worked in the court, teaching the king through tricks. But there is another tradition, as elsewhere, of clever young boys who, had wit and played effective tricks, just as the boy did here with the water buffalo.

The boy trickster—sometimes anonymous, sometimes named—is found throughout the world. A similar well-known American character is Jack, while A-Chey in Cambodia is also often portrayed as a youth. Another famous young trickster is the novice priest, Ikkyusan, in Japan. As a boy, he also often tricked someone in authority—the priest.

Why the Water Buffalo Can't

Once in Vietnam, a young boy took care of a farmer's water buffalo. Every day, he went to a field where other boys gathered. There he tied the buffalo to a tree. Then he and his friends played battle games with flags and sticks. But soon the grass around the tree was all eaten up. And the buffalo grew weaker and thinner. Finally one day the boy noticed the change.

"I'll be in terrible trouble if the farmer finds out about this," he thought. While he worried, he chanced upon a plan. Quickly, he gathered the husks of some betel nuts. He wet them well. Next he pasted them on the water buffalo and sculpted a nice, rounded shape. Finally, he plastered rich mud all over the animal, to hold everything in place. Satisfied, he beamed at the water buffalo. The animal now looked healthy and plump, all covered in mud, as a water buffalo should be.

That night, the buffalo, although he appeared full, felt very, very hungry. When the farmer walked by, the buffalo bellowed, "***I'm starvingggggg.***"

"You can't be, just look at you," replied the farmer.

"That's not really me," said the animal. "Touch my side and see."

When the farmer discovered the boy's trick, he punished him at once. From then on, the boy had to feed the water buffalo and watch him closely all day, so he couldn't play with his friends any more. He grew very bored, then angry. It seemed that the buffalo's huge eyes were always laughing at him.

So one day he took his revenge. When the water buffalo was sleeping, the boy crept up holding two incense sticks. All at once, he pressed them both into the animal's chin, making two small round marks.

Much surprised, the water buffalo awoke and opened his mouth. But no sounds came out. He tried to call the farmer. Yet there was only silence. He could not speak. Since that day, water buffaloes have had small spots on their chins. And never again have they been able to say even one word!

Telling Tips for "Why the Water Buffalo Can't Talk"

This tale has several distinct characters, so you can use a little acting and slight voice changes to give them each a flavor. The water buffalo should be slow talking and moving, while the boy would probably be quick to speak and act, and the farmer can be as you wish him.

If you like to mime, you can take your time to show how the boy patted on the betel nut and mud to make the buffalo bigger. Practice slowly patting it on so that the audience really believes you and starts to see it themselves.

When the water buffalo tries to talk at the end of tale, he must be very frustrated. See if you can convey some of that feeling using your facial expressions.

Activities

1. The water buffalo is a very important animal in Asia and elsewhere. Check out the web site and links below, then work in small groups to make colorful posters about the animal. Divide up assignments and include a drawing, traits and habits, a map showing settings, a description of habitats, and more.
2. This is an interesting story to think and write about. The boy played a mean trick on the buffalo. What if the story continued after the trick? What would be a fair ending to trick the boy back, or to make him pay in some way for his deed? Share your thoughts in a class discussion or with some writing that shows a different ending.
3. Since there are many images in this story, it could make an interesting picture book. In partners, design an 8–12 page book combining pictures and simple text. You can retell the story from several perspectives: using a storyteller's voice, in the words of the boy or the farmer, or from the viewpoint of the poor water buffalo himself.

Resources

Chase, Richard. *The Jack Tales.* Houghton Mifflin, 1993. A great collection of the boy Jack's many tricks in the Southeastern United States.

Mayer, Fanny Hagin, ed. *Ancient Tales in Modern Japan.* Indiana University Press, 1984. Includes several Ikkyusan tales.

Water Buffalo Site *http://ww2.netnitco.net/user/djiligda/waterbuf.htm*

A website which includes many links to scientific studies, water buffalo projects worldwide, and pictures.

Chapter 12

Korea

"The Farmer and the Tokaebi"

Kim Sondal is a trickster from long-ago Korea. However, many of his tales are a bit longer and harder to share with younger listeners. So here is a trick played by a quick-witted farmer against a well-known Korean monster, the tokaebi. The tokaebi seems related to the Japanese oni—he is large, strong, and fierce-looking—but in stories, he can also be tricked and fooled.

Tokaebi *pronounced DOE-KAY-BEE*

The Farmer and the Tokaebi

Long ago in Korea, there lived a farmer and his wife. One night, they sat eating rice and kimchee in their cozy house. But all of a sudden, they heard frightening screams and felt the ground shake.

"What is that?" cried the wife, much afraid.

"I don't know," said the husband, equally scared. "But the noises are getting louder. And they seem to be coming from our front yard."

Standing up slowly, he walked to the door and opened it a crack. He peeked out and saw huge, fierce tokaebi monsters. They were dancing, shouting, and fighting, right in front of his house. Suddenly, he wasn't scared any more, he was mad.

"***Go away, you tokaebi!***" he shouted. "***This is our house.***"

"***Ha, ha, ha!***" cried the biggest tokaebi. "This is ***not*** your place, it is ours."

"You are wrong. Leave right now!" ordered the farmer. But the tokaebi kept jumping and dancing.

"***Get off my land!***" shouted the farmer, stamping his feet.

"You say it's yours, I say it's ours," said the biggest tokaebi. "So let's have a contest. Whoever wins gets to keep the house. Whoever loses, has to leave."

Now this seemed most unfair to the farmer, since it was his house. But it's hard to fight with someone very big and very frightening. So the farmer nodded and said, "We'll each give one problem for this contest. You start."

The tokaebi rubbed his horns and thought for a while. Then he asked,

"How many bowls would it take to empty the sea?"

"That depends on the size of the bowl," answered the farmer right away. "If you had an enormous bowl, then only one bowl would be needed. If you had a bowl half that size, then you would need two!"

Much annoyed at the farmer's clever answer, the tokaebi roared, "***All right, you win that. But, our contest is not over. Now, you ask me a question.***"

The farmer then walked to the door of his home. He opened the door and stepped right over the doorstep, with one foot outside the house and one foot inside. He placed one arm outside and one inside. He turned his face so that it looked neither out nor in.

"Am I going in or am I going out?" he asked. Of course the tokaebi did not know what to say. Whatever he said would be wrong. The tokaebi's face grew redder and redder. His arms waved madly about, his feet pounded the ground. But he had promised—so finally, along with his tokaebi friends, he stomped away. Thus at last, the clever farmer and his wife were left in the peace they well deserved.

Telling Tips for "The Farmer and the Tokaebi"

This is a great tale for sound effects. The sounds of the tokaebi leaping, growling, and stomping are lots of fun to share. You can also show the farmer's mood changing from rather scared to very angry as he tries to chase away the monsters. Decide if you want to give the tokaebi some gesture while he thinks: shaking his big head, scratching his hair, etc. When the farmer asks his riddle, you can physically show how he stands, with one hand in and one out, etc. That way, your audience will more clearly understand how impossible a question it is.

Activities

1. Riddles go well with storytelling, as in this tale. Many folktales include a riddle challenge to a prospective bride or groom, to a king or noble, or to a wise minister. Traditional riddles usually either 1) describe the attributes of the object ("Animal with two tails: elephant") or 2) use metaphor, naming characteristics of one object while referring to another with similar attributes ("Red snake wandering amidst white stones: tongue"). Exchange riddles in class, finding more, if needed, in sources below. If you'd like, divide your class in half and have a riddle contest.
2. There are many monsters and beings around the world, tricking or being tricked, scaring or being scared. Try to find a range of such beings in library references. Work in partners, and have each pair contribute one monster sheet for a class book. On each sheet have an illustration and the name of the monster with relevant details: physical description, setting, lifestyle, weapons used, etc. Or you could each make big "Wanted" posters to decorate the hall. If you have access to a video camera, you could make this idea come alive on a video!

3. Put the tokaebi in a modern city and have him trespassing, just as he is in this story. Then fill out a police report, stating: date, location, victim, incident, witnesses, and how the incident was resolved.

Resources

Han, Suzanne Crowder. *Korean Folk & Fairy Tales.* Hollym, 1991. A fine source of Korean tales, including several with the tokaebi.

NIEHS Kids' Pages *www.niehs.nih.gov/kids/braint.htm*

Exciting site for kids, full of riddles and brainteasers.

Young, Ed. *High on a Hill.* Collins, 1980. Lovely picture book of traditional Chinese riddles.

Hmong

"Monkey Thieves"

Shao
pronounced
SH-OU (as is out)

In the Hmong tradition, found in Laos and China, a character named Orphan can sometimes play tricks, in often longer tales. In this brief tale, it is Shao, a spiritual being important to the Hmong, who gives the trick to play, and the farmer who simply follows directions. But Shao is not a heavenly trickster: in another well known Hmong tale, *Nine in-One, Grr! Grr!,* Shao can't think up a trick, so a little black bird helps out and manages to trick a tiger.

Monkey Thieves

Long ago in Laos, a lazy farmer found a few rice grains.

"I'm hungry," he thought, "so, I guess I'll plant this rice." But, since he was very, very lazy, he simply sat for a long time, just thinking about work.

After a while, his hunger made him move. He walked to a nearby field. He cut down some trees and slowly smoothed the ground. Then he threw the rice grains this way and that. Afterwards, very tired, he dragged himself back home to sleep.

Day by day, the sun helped the rice to grow. Day by day, the rain helped the rice to grow. But the farmer didn't help the rice at all. He only slept, dreaming rice dreams. Finally one morning he thought, "My rice must be ripe by now." And he went happily to pick it. Yet when he saw his field, he stopped suddenly, his mouth wide open.

"My rice is all gone!" he shouted, staring at the empty field. "Who stole it?" The farmer searched everywhere for some sign of the thief. Bending down, all at once he saw... fresh tracks.

"Monkeys!" he cried, "Monkey thieves!" The farmer shook his fists, wondering what to do.

"I'll ask the great Shao up above," he thought after awhile. "He is clever and kind. He will help." Off went the farmer, to climb the great ladder which led to Shao's home in the sky.

"Oh wise Shao," the man called into the clouds which hid Shao. "The monkeys ate all my rice. I'm hungry and I want to teach them a lesson. What can I do?" At first, only silence circled round. Then, slowly, a voice spoke. "Find some sweet bananas. Lay down near the field, and put them all over your body. Wait, and don't move—until you feel the monkeys right next to you. Then, give them a big surprise."

Down the ladder returned the farmer, thinking about Shao's strange words. "I'll try his idea," thought the farmer, "since I don't have any other. And besides, I am very good at lying down." Back on the ground, he found many ripe bananas, covered himself up, and almost fell asleep. Then he heard new sounds nearby.

"Look at the strange banana plant!" chattered some monkeys. "What is it, what is it? Maybe a new plant that grows on the ground. Call our friends. Let's have a feast!"

Word of the weird banana plant flew through the trees. Monkeys, big and small, quickly gathered, with loads of nuts, fruits, and sugarcane. They scattered food all around the banana plant. They bounced up and down and licked hungry lips.

Next, with tails and toes hopping, the monkeys began to dance. Closer and closer they jumped around the man. But he stayed very, very still. He didn't move at all. Closer and closer, they kept on dancing, yet he remained silent. Closer and closer they came to the man, until...

"***Ahhhhhh!***" Up he jumped with a roar, scaring them all. Monkeys leapt into trees, scrambled through leaves, and fled from that scary banana plant.

Satisfied, the farmer looked down at the monkeys' food. He yawned, tired after all his work. He rested for a while. Then he picked up the fresh treasures and strolled back home.

Now the lazy farmer could sleep all he wanted, yet he still had so much to eat... at least for a while. Later, after all the food was finished, maybe that lazy farmer would work a little harder to grow some more.

And then again, maybe he would not.

Telling Tips for "Monkey Thieves"

Try to make the farmer quite lazy—by your voice and even your actions. When he talks to Shao, you can show Shao's deeper, more mysterious voice. If you are telling to little children, you could add a simple repeated chant at the end as the monkeys circle closer and closer. Children love such repetition, even with the simplest melody, with words like, "This will taste so good," or even, "We're hungry, so hungry."

The sudden jump and cry of the farmer can be used to surprise any audience. Lower your voice a little right before it, to trick your audience a bit, so that they don't expect a big sound. Then shout out and jump a bit too, with your hands toward the listeners. You might even make a few listeners jump themselves!

Activities

1. The surprise at the end makes this story a natural for a pop-up book or card. Use the resources below or search for another in your library to help you learn how to make pop-ups (using paper springs, cuttings, etc.). On the outside of the card or beginning of the book, write the story or draw pictures in sequence. Then make a final pop-up of the farmer springing up and scaring the monkeys.
2. Keeping animals away from crops is a problem around the world. Working alone or with partners, invent a way to keep monkeys out of a field. Challenge yourselves to try two inventions: 1) using resources available to a subsistence farmer in a small village in Laos, and 2) high-tech materials available to a rich farmer in the future.

Resources

Livo, Norma. *Folk Stories of the Hmong.* Libraries Unlimited, 1991. Lovely collection of Hmong tales and photos, with cultural background.

Robson, Denny. *Paper Craft.* Gloucester Press, 1993. Includes directions for origami flowers and for pop-up cards.

Xiong, Blia and Cathy Spagnoli. *Nine-in-One, Grr! Grr!* Children's Book Press, 1989. A fun trick, with a chant that listeners love to echo.

Chapter 14

India

"The Well"

Tenali Raman, whose name can be spelled several different ways, is beloved in South India. He was a wit in the court of the famous Raja Krishna Deva Raya. Tenali Raman played many tricks on the raja, while also protecting the kingdom with his wit (through solutions to challenges from neighboring rulers). Many Indians still know his stories today; they are shared by telling, in books, through comics, and on television. But he remains a historical trickster, based on legend, and so there are no new tales about him.

Tenali Raman *pronounced TEH-NAL-EE RAH-MAHN*

It was said that he got his wit and cunning through a blessing from the Goddess Kali herself. After tricking his way into the palace, he often made the other court advisors quite jealous, and he enjoyed outwitting them as well.

In northern India, another court wit is widely known: Birbal, who was in the court of the great Emperor Akbar. The stories of both men overlap; more tales of both can be found in the resources below.

The Well

Once in India, clever Tenali Raman spied two thieves hiding near his house. He quickly thought of a plan. In a loud voice he called to his wife, "Wife, I've heard that there are thieves around. Let us put all our jewels in a trunk and hide it in the well."

His wife, quite surprised, started to say that they had no jewels. But she saw her husband signaling her to agree. So, she replied loudly, "What a good idea." The two then noisily filled a trunk with bits of pots and bricks. Next, with grunts and groans, they pushed it out of the house and into the well. The trunk made a fine splash and the two went back inside. Soon after, Tenali Raman crept out to spy on the thieves.

"How easy they have made it for us," said a pleased thief. "Now we will just empty the well and take the trunk. Then we'll have all their treasure without any risk."

Eagerly, the thieves started to pull the bucket up and down in order to empty the well. Bucket after bucket of water was splashed all over the ground. Tenali Raman watched very happily as the water flowed away from the well and down the ditches that watered his plants.

After hours and hours of this hard work, the thieves had emptied most of the well. And Tenali Raman's plants were nicely watered. So he called out, "Thank you so much, my friends, for watering my plants. Now please wait, for the palace guards will come soon to arrest you."

When the thieves heard those words, they ran off in separate ways and never returned. Tenali Raman went inside, well pleased, with his garden well watered, and had a fine night's sleep.

Telling Tips for "The Well"

Use some exaggerated movements as Tenali Raman talks loudly but gestures to his wife. If you like to use gestures, this is a great story for you. Show the struggle as Tenali Raman and his wife carry the trunk out. Then mime the thieves emptying bucket after bucket. Finally, make Tenali Raman's voice very cheerful as he thanks the thieves at the end! If you'd like to try an Indian storytelling technique, use collaboration and drama. Tell the tale in a small group, using a narrator-teller and several actors.

Activities

1. Tenali Raman is a great favorite in South India. In this trick, he solved his problem of watering the garden, while also tricking the thieves. Working in partners, see if you can create a story which also "kills two birds with one stone."
2. This would be a fun story to make a model of, using your choice of materials: Legos, cardboard, folded paper, etc. Include the well, a loaded trunk, and perhaps even water draining into plants.

Resources

Beck, Brenda, et al., eds. *Folktales of India.* University of Chicago Press, 1987. Part of the excellent folk tale series from the University of Chicago.

Ramanujan, A. K., ed. 1991. *Folktales from India.* Pantheon. A rich collection by a well known Indian scholar/poet.

Spagnoli, Cathy, and Paramasivam Samanna. *Jasmine and Coconuts: South Indian Tales.* Libraries Unlimited, 1999. This introduction to South India includes tales of Tenali Raman.

Chapter 15

Nepal

"A Goblin's Trick"

There are many tales of tricks in Nepal, but tales of traditional tricksters are harder to find. This tale shares a trick answered by a trick, and includes a well known character around the world—the goblin. The tale's theme—of a kind neighbor rewarded, a greedy neighbor punished—is one echoed throughout Asia and elsewhere, for most cultures still teach that "greed does not pay."

A Goblin's Trick

Once upon a time in Nepal, travelers stopped at an inn named Marusatal. One evening, a kind old woman, with three big goiters on her neck, came to the inn.

Marusatal *pronounced MAH-ROO-A-TAHL*

Now that morning, the woman had made four fine rice cakes for her journey. While traveling, she shared two with a friend. The other two she wrapped in her sash, to keep for breakfast. Then she folded it up for a pillow and soon fell asleep.

That night, a goblin appeared—a goblin with magical powers. He came to the place where she slept and stared at her. In the soft light, her goiters looked like lovely jewels. He liked them very, very much. So all at once, he took them and put them on his own neck.

He looked again at the woman. He saw the two rice cakes hidden under her head. Since they looked so delicious, the goblin took them too. But, being a fair goblin, he left two golden cakes in exchange.

When the woman woke up the next morning, her neck felt so light. Very curious, she touched her neck and found her goiters gone. She washed her face with great joy, and then looked for her rice cakes. They were missing too, but in their place she found two golden cakes. Amazed at her good luck, she ran back to her village—with two precious cakes and without the pesky goiters. Back home, she shared her wealth, for her heart was a good one.

Soon, her greedy neighbor came over. "How did you get rich? And where are your goiters?" she asked, since she had four annoying goiters herself. The kind woman happily told her. At once, the greedy neighbor decided to go to the same place.

"But I shall trick whoever comes at night," she thought. "I'll put ten cakes made of old husks under my pillow, so that I'll get more wealth." Quickly, she made some rough, tasteless cakes and rushed to Marusatal.

While she slept, the goblin came. Although tired now of the goiters, he was still hungry, so he tasted a cake. ***"Ucchh!"*** He spit it out, most annoyed.

"She tried to trick me," he thought. "Well, I'll trick her." With a wave of his goblin hand, his three goiters flew over to stick on her neck. Then he left, without touching the rest of those awful cakes.

Early the next morning, the woman had trouble lifting her head. And she looked under her pillow only to find the same old cakes. So, with a heavy heart and a heavy neck, she returned slowly and sadly to her home.

Telling Tips for "A Goblin's Trick"

This is quite a straightforward tale. The strongest character is the greedy woman. You can show her eagerness to get rich, and her rather sloppy, quick way of making the cakes. Of course, it is nice to share the joy and surprise of the kind woman when she touches her light neck. The goblin could be shown in a slightly ghostly manner, if you wish. You could play with your voice as you tell about him, slowing it down and making it a little strange. Don't overdo it, though, because the story is short, and in this story, the goblin is not really a scary goblin.

Activities

1. If you'd like to have some fun after this story, consider the rice cakes the women made. One was quite delicious, although plain, the other quite terrible to taste. Make up two recipes for cakes of some sort: one good and one bad, listing ingredients and steps to make each one. Try to make the good one actually good enough to eat!
2. "Greed Does Not Pay" is the theme of this story and of many others around the world. It is still an important message today. Create a poster, for a modern audience, that discourages greed using a saying, a picture, or a cartoon.

Resources

Shrestha, Kavita and Sarah Lamstein. *From the Mango Tree and Other Folktales From Nepal.* Libraries Unlimited, 1997. One of the few collections of tales from Nepal; includes a trick tale or two.

Chapter 16

Indonesia

"A Strange Bird"

Although Sang Kancil is found in Indonesia, West Java's popular trickster is Si Kabayan. He is a farmer who can be tricky one moment and a fool the next. Unlike some tricksters, who remain in one era or historical time frame, Si Kabayan has moved with the times. Tales of his tricks are set both in the distant past and in modern times. There are tales told, for example, of what happened when Si Kabayan met the Dutch rulers of Indonesia in this century.

Sang Kancil *pronounced SAHNG KAHN-CHEEL*

Si Kabayan *pronounced SEE KAH-BAH-YAHN*

Like many tricksters, he uses verbal wit quite often, and he can change effortlessly from boasting to blabbering. His sense of self-preservation carries him in and out of situations, allowing him to read people and switch tactics as needed. Si Kabayan most often tricks those in his village environment; he is not seen as often with royalty, as some other tricksters are.

A Strange Bird

On the lovely island of Java in Indonesia, Si Kabayan once lived and played tricks. One day, he had to fool the village moneylender. You see, Si Kabayan owed money he couldn't repay. To get ready, Si Kabayan covered himself with palm oil. Then he rolled around in the soft downy feathers left by his chickens.

Next he built a large bamboo cage, gave his wife a few directions, and stepped into it. His wife quickly covered it with an old batik cloth, then went to greet the moneylender. She served him fresh mango and papaya and sighed.

"I'm so sorry," she said. "But my husband is not home."

"Where is he now?" scowled the moneylender.

"He's gone to see the king."

"Whatever for?" he asked.

"Well, yesterday in the forest he caught an extraordinary bird. He will sell it to the king for a large sum."

"Ahhhh, I would like to see that bird," suggested the greedy moneylender.

"It's caged here now," said the wife. "And Si Kabayan gave me strict orders not to let anyone near it."

"Please let me take a peek," begged the moneylender. "I lent you money."

"But, you might scare the bird if you look," the wife argued.

"Just a little look," he pleaded. Still she refused.

Yet the moneylender begged and pleaded, pleaded and begged...

...until she finally agreed. She took him to the cage and lifted the cloth. All at once, with a strange ***"Aaakkk"*** a feathered being leapt into some nearby bamboo.

"What happened?" shouted the moneylender, staring at the empty cage.

"Look what you've done!" sobbed the wife. "The bird has escaped! What will my husband say? What will the king do?"

"Please don't mention my name," begged the moneylender. "I don't need trouble."

"But what can I do?" cried the wife.

"Just tell the king some child did it. If you do, I'll wipe out your debt. You will not owe me a thing."

"I'm not sure," hesitated the wife. "That bird was soooo rare. The king would have given us much money and honor."

"Please help me this time," begged the moneylender.

"Well... you did loan us some money and you meant no harm," said the wife slowly. "***Oh, all right!*** We'll trade your good name for our debt."

Greatly relieved, the moneylender left, never to return. And soon after that, Si Kabayan returned from the forest. He washed off his feathers and grinned proudly at his wife.

Then the two sat down to celebrate. And soon after that, Si Kabayan started to plan his next trick!

Telling Tips for "A Strange Bird"

The moneylender has a nasty sort of character—one minute very demanding and the next minute whining and pleading to see the bird. If you can show this by your face and the feeling in your voice, then do. The wife can be portrayed rather simply: she is just doing what she was told to do, and perhaps is not quite sure why. When the bird does escape, feel free to add some strange squawks and flapping or "bird-running" sounds.

If you like making props, and are telling to younger audiences, then try making a model of the strange bird. You can have fun designing it out of feathers, pieces of cotton, cloth, whatever. Use it as you tell the tale, keeping it covered mysteriously, then quickly showing it and hiding it again.

Activities

1. Si Kabayan used his trick to get out of debt. Was that fair? Consider first the high rate of interest charged by many moneylenders, especially in some parts of the world. (Use math to figure out how much one would owe if the moneylender charged 20% interest. How about 50%?) Then debate the question.
2. Si Kabayan created this rare bird. In Indonesia, if he wanted to use a real rare bird, what would he use? How about in Spain? West Africa? Where you live? In the library or on the Internet, look for lists and descriptions of endangered birds, then spread the word of those in danger through a poster or drawing.

Resources

Armstrong, Beverly. *Endangered Animals.* The Learning Works, 1994. Creative art ideas centered around endangered animals.

Spagnoli, Cathy. *Treasury of Asian Stories and Activities for Schools and Libraries.* Alleyside, 1998. Includes another Si Kabayan story.

Malaysia

"The Stolen Scents"

Sang Kancil
pronounced
SAHNG KAHN-CHEEL

Here is another of the many tales about the popular trickster Sang Kancil. In this one, he moves out of his jungle home and into the world of humans. As he does, he seems related to Judge Rabbit, who felt equally at home helping animals or helping people. Though Sang Kancil helps humans here, most of his stories pit him against a jungle creature. In the rich, ancient jungles of Malaysia and Indonesia, there are indeed many powerful creatures to trick.

The Stolen Scents

Long ago in Malaysia, a poor couple lived next to a rich merchant. One day, the poor man's wife spoke to one of her friends.

"We dine very well at our house," she said. "We only eat when our rich neighbors are cooking or frying. In that way, the delicious smells make our simple rice taste better."

Well, the friend told HER friend, who told someone else... and soon the rich man's wife heard. She was furious.

"Dear husband," she said. "No wonder we don't have good health. Those greedy neighbors have stolen our cooking smells for years and years."

"Terrible, wife, just terrible," sighed the merchant. "They should pay us for all that they've taken."

"What a clever idea," said the wife. "Bring our neighbor here at once and demand our money." So the rich merchant summoned the poor man.

"For too long you have used our smells," said the merchant. "So you must now pay for years of cooking supplies, and for our cook's wages as well."

"But that is not fair," protested the poor man. "We never touched your food. We only took the smells which the air carried freely to us." Yet the greedy rich man kept on insisting. At last, he took his case to the sultan.

The sultan listened to the rich man's demand. He listened to the poor man's defense. Finally, the sultan shook his head, unable to decide. He sent a messenger throughout the land, declaring, "Whoever can decide the case of the stolen scents will be well rewarded."

Word spread across the land, but no one came forward. Until little Sang Kancil, the clever mousedeer, heard of the problem. He pranced into the palace to offer his skill. The two men were soon brought before him and he listened to their pleas.

"Did you ever go inside the rich man's house?" he asked the poor neighbor.

"Never," replied the man.

"Did you ever go inside his garden?"

"Never."

"Did you ever taste even one bite of his food?"

"No, sir, not even one tiny lick," the man answered. Then Sang Kancil turned to the rich man and asked, "How much do you think he owes you for all the smells he's enjoyed?"

"The cost of materials and labor over the years comes to 1,000 gold coins," said the rich man loudly. Sang Kancil then borrowed 1,000 coins from the sultan.

"Go stand with these coins behind that curtain," he ordered the poor man. "Let your neighbor stand on the other side. Then please count the coins loudly."

The poor man counted the money, as the merchant listened greedily. When the counting was done, Sang Kancil said to the rich man, "That, sir, is a full and complete settlement of your account."

"Thank you," said the rich man. "That is indeed the proper sum. Please give me the coins now, and I will have them carried to my home."

"Dear sir," said Sang Kancil. "These coins are not for you. They belong to the sultan. Your account is already settled. Your neighbor took the worth of 1,000 coins by smelling, and you have received them back by hearing."

So, as the poor man walked off grinning and the rich man fuming, Sang Kancil went happily home to rest.

Telling Tips for "The Stolen Scents"

Find the voice and gestures you wish to portray the mousedeer as he acts as a judge. Add a royal gesture to define the sultan's order, and show his frustration, too. If you like to call out, have the royal crier sound his message loudly and slowly—perhaps with a loud clap, like a drum. Decide how you wish to portray the rich man and his wife. Will she be loud and shrew-like or rather proud and snobby? Will he be too mean and greedy? End with his anger if you like to use expression.

Activities

1. This particular trick is very popular in many cultures. Using the library resources below, find as many versions as possible. Then make a mural, with one picture from each student. Each illustration should show a version of the trick, with the title and relevant details written.
2. Imagine your favorite meals for a week. Total up approximate costs, multiply by 52 weeks in a year, and then by 10 years. If you were to charge someone for all that food, how much would they owe?
3. The mousedeer is a fascinating animal because of its miniature size. Locate a drawing or photo of this tiny deer and then try to make your own drawing or model of him, placing him in his setting of the rich Malay jungle.

Resources

Carpenter, Frances. *The Elephant's Bathtub.* Doubleday, 1962. This collection boasts a version from Cambodia of the stolen scents.

Spagnoli, Cathy. *Asian Tales and Tellers.* August House, 1998. In this anthology, Princess Learned-in-the-Law helps a poor man accused of stealing smells.

Yolen, Jane, ed. *Favorite Folktales From Around the World.* Pantheon, 1986. In this rich collection, Jane Yolen shares a version from Africa.

Chapter 18

China

"Lazy Dragon at the Inn"

Lazy Dragon is a thief who plays tricks. He is a likable character, even though he's a thief, since—like Robin Hood—he steals from the greedy rich and gives to the needy poor. Lazy Dragon has a strict code of honor along with great daring. His name suits him: he is called "lazy," not because he is actually lazy, but because he sleeps during the day and works at night. And he is called "dragon," because, like the dragons of old Chinese tales, he can transform himself. He is a master of disguises; he can change his appearance, his voice, or his walk. And he is skilled in the ways of the thief: quick and quiet, able to climb, to enter locked places, and to hide well.

Lazy Dragon often painted a small plum blossom, left behind to claim credit for a theft. And he especially loved to fool the rich, as well as corrupt officials. His tales were told by various Chinese storytellers long ago, along with the popular tales of tricky foxes. Many Chinese storytellers still share famous tricks from Chinese Classics (like the long tale of the popular trickster Monkey). Several other styles of storytelling feature comic telling, with cunning men playing tricks on those in high

Lazy Dragon at the Inn

One day, Lazy Dragon was sitting in a restaurant with his good friend. The two were sharing tales about Lazy Dragon's adventures.

As they laughed and laughed, the innkeeper grew curious. He came, listened, and finally spoke, "Lazy Dragon, if you are such a good thief, can you steal from me?"

"I could try," said Lazy Dragon, who loved a challenge.

"You see this vase," said the innkeeper as he held up a lovely vase, thin at the neck, but wide at the base. "I'll bet that you can't take it from me tonight. If you can, I'll feed you for a year."

Lazy Dragon smiled quietly and agreed. Then he went home to plan. Later that night, he walked back to the inn. On the way, he stopped at a butcher's shop, a tailor's shop, and a stall with building supplies.

When he got to the inn, he saw that it was all locked up. And he was in luck, for inside the building, the innkeeper was sleeping with his head on a table. In the middle of the table was the vase.

Lazy Dragon looked at the roof and saw sparkling tiles, with a tiny chimney. He knew that the tiles were supported by wood slats too close together for a body to slip through. But Lazy Dragon had a plan. What do you think he did?

(Storytellers: Pause for all kinds of answers, and if needed, remind listeners that you gave them some clues. Then go on...)

Well, he went on the roof and took off some tiles that were above the vase. Now, ***he*** couldn't fit through, but the vase could come UP. So next he took a piece of bamboo. Then he pulled out a pig's bladder. Why? Well, a pig's bladder works like a balloon, and that's what he wanted.

He tied the bladder to the end of the bamboo with some thread. Then he slowly lowered it down until it went right inside the vase. Next, he carefully blew and blew and blew... until the bladder filled up the bottom of the vase, holding it.

When it felt secure, he quickly stuffed the top of the bamboo with cloth, to keep the air in. Then he slowly pulled the vase up and climbed down to the ground.

The next day he went to the inn and knocked on the door. When the innkeeper came, Lazy Dragon held out the vase and said, "Here's your vase. And I'm very hungry..."

Telling Tips for "Lazy Dragon at the Inn"

This is almost a detective story, especially if you let listeners guess how Lazy Dragon plays his trick. Make sure that you give all of the hints in the story (e.g., the stores he passes, etc.), but don't go overboard and give them too much emphasis. When you get to the actual theft, do pause as the text suggests. Let listeners give responses. Accept all answers in a positive way, even if they aren't the traditional ones. You'll probably have time to hear about four or five ideas. If by that time you have heard the right one, just repeat it loudly to all. Or, as often happens, if someone gives part of the answer, then build upon that and finish it. If no one is very close, then just cheerfully thank them and go on with the right answer and finish the story.

When Lazy Dragon goes to steal the vase, it's nice to mime lowering the bamboo, blowing into it slowly, plugging the hole, and then carefully pulling up the vase. You can finish with a nice knock on the door at the end; then hold the vase out while looking hungry.

Activities

1. Search for more tricky thieves in the resources below. Then as a class, brainstorm the types of tricks that Lazy Dragon could play as he steals from the greedy rich to help the needy poor. Place him in the present, in any setting, and make up a few relevant tricks. Include his training as a thief and his skills of disguise in some of the tricks. Don't forget how resourceful he is: able to use materials close at hand when needed, whether high- or low-tech!
2. This type of character might not be accepted by everyone. Perhaps some people would feel that being a thief, in any way, for any reason, is wrong. Write two short news articles (or letters) about this trick. Write the first as if you really admire Lazy Dragon's character; write the second as if you disapprove.

Resources

McNeill, James. *The Double Knights: More Tales From Round the World.* Oxford University Press, 1984. Another tale of a clever thief, who tricks a king.

Waley, Arthur. *Dear Monkey.* Bobbs-Merrill, 1973. A noted translation of the famous epic, starring Monkey.

Yang, Xianyi and Gladys Yang. *The Courtesan's Jewel Box.* Foreign Languages Press, 1981 A source for more Lazy Dragon tales; best for older readers.

Pakistan

"Trust"

The most well known trickster in Islamic countries is definitely Hodja, known also as Nasruddin Hodja, or the Mullah, and by other names. He is a combination of a fool and a wise man. Since his tales are quite widely available (see Resources), here instead is a tale of a woman's wit. In the Islamic tradition, there are a number of learned women as well as clever girls and housewives. This example of a woman's wit is especially nice, since she fools a greedy but respected judge who should know better!

Trust

Once in an Eastern land, there lived a poor ragpicker. He worked hard, doing a dirty job, and saving his pitiful wages. Every day as he worked, he dreamt of returning to his family home far away. After years and years of such weary toil, he had saved a bag of coins.

"I must keep this very safe," he thought. "Then I shall work a few more years and at last return home." He decided that the safest place would be with a chief judge in the city. He went to the palace and bowed before the man.

"Sir," he begged. "Would you please guard my earnings for the next few years?" The judge agreed and had the bag taken away.

Soon after that, the poor man heard that some traders were going to his homeland. He suddenly decided to join them, for it seemed a good chance to go home. Eagerly, he ran to the judge and asked for his money.

"Money?" shouted the judge. "What money, you wicked liar? Who are you cheating? I should have you thrown in prison. Get out of here now and I'll spare your miserable life."

In great sorrow and frustration, the poor man left, chased by the guards. He could not go home empty-handed, and felt worse than ever, facing years and years of terrible toil.

One day soon after, he picked up some rags in front of a fine home. Without thinking, he sighed with such sorrow that it touched the woman who lived there. She called to him and asked why he was so sad. He slowly told her how he had been cheated. She was furious and promised to help him.

"Let me talk to the judge," she said. "I shall go early tomorrow. You come at noon to the palace and ask for your money."

The next morning, she dressed in her richest clothes and put on fine scents. She gathered her best jewels into a cloth, and then spoke to her servant.

"When you see the ragpicker come out of the judge's room, then I want you to run in, saying, 'Your husband has returned and awaits you.'"

Some time later, the lovely lady stood before the judge.

"Kind sir," she said. "My husband remains in Egypt and I wish to go join him there. However, it is not safe to take my jewels with me. Can I trust you to guard them?"

The judge looked at the sparkling gems and was about to reply when the ragpicker ran suddenly into the room.

"Sir, please give me my money back now," he requested. "I have found some companions to journey with." The judge turned to his servant, and said, "Bring the man's bag at once."

As the coins of the poor man were handed over, the judge spoke to the rich woman, "You see how my people trust me. I have kept this poor soul's few coins faithfully. I will also carefully watch your jewels."

With a bow, the poor man left happily, holding his treasure. As soon as he left, the woman's servant ran into the room.

"Mistress, mistress," he cried. "Come at once. Your husband has suddenly returned and awaits you."

"What wondrous news," she said and gathered up all of her jewels. She bid the judge farewell and hurried away.

The judge sat for some time in confusion, very sorry that the jewels were gone. But at last he laughed and said to himself, "I have been a judge for 40 years. And never before has a case been won in such a clever way."

Telling Tips for "Trust"

You have a chance in this tale to portray sadness. The disappointment and quiet frustration of the man can come out. If you feel brave enough, a sad moan, or a chant, or a bit of a song could help to convey his sorrow after his loss. The judge can be portrayed with a voice and action showing his harshness at times, as well as his false goodness. The kindness and good heart of the woman can be shown with a gesture or soft expression. And the excited cry of her servant should be well heard, since it signals the happy ending of the tale.

Activities

1. Although this woman is not a trickster with a series of tricks told about her, she does play a good trick. Since there aren't enough such female tricksters, as a class, create a female trickster. Here are some of the things you should consider:
   - her appearance
   - her age
   - language spoken
   - the setting
   - her background
   - types of tricks she does, with several examples.
2. Tape recording stories is great fun. Some stories sound better than others, especially those with sound effects. This would be a nice, simple one to tape: it has a varied cast and possibilities for sound effects. Try taping it in small groups and compare results.

Resources

Nasruddin Hodja

http://w1.871.telia.com/~u87109316/index_eng.htm Here is a whole website dedicated to Hodja!

Walker, Barbara K. *Watermelons, Walnuts, and the Wisdom of Allah, and Other Tales of the Hoca.* Texas Tech University Press, 1991. Use this to share more tales of the popular trickster Hodja.

Chapter 20

Cambodia

"Judge Rabbit and the Strange Creature"

Judge Rabbit is a favorite trickster in Cambodia. He lives in the forest, likes to munch cucumbers, and to think quickly. He is an interesting character, for although he enjoys tricking more powerful creatures, like the tiger and some humans, he also likes to help men and women. He is indeed a judge, and frequently decides cases after a human judge has been unable to decide the case fairly.

There is a large, well known cycle of tales about Judge Rabbit. He tricks farmers and crocodiles, kings and elephants. And he is himself tricked by some snails who work together to win a race. Yet his heart is a good one, and he helps many, especially the weak. In fact, he was so well-regarded in Cambodia, that they say the seal of the chief magistrate contained a picture of this trickster-hero.

Judge Rabbit and the Strange Creature

Once in Cambodia, two merchants went to trade in a far-off city. That night, they found themselves in a dark forest. A bit scared, they prepared to sleep.

"I want to sleep in the middle," said one, "it's safest."

"No, I do," said the other. But then they realized that there was no middle with just two people.

"I know," said one, "let us put the soles of our feet together. That way, we'll feel more safe." So they touched toes and stretched out in opposite directions, making a long line of their bodies. Then they covered themselves completely with a big cloth.

Soon their snores tore through the night. A tiger came to see what was making the noise. He stared at the strange shape.

"IT has no head or tail, IT looks all the same except for the bumps at both ends," he thought. "IT may be dangerous, even though it is quiet now. I better go warn the others."

Off he ran, and soon, one by one, all the animals came and stared at the strange creature.

"***It*** could be a fish," said a deer, "but fish don't sleep here."

"***It*** looks like my relatives, but without eyes," said a python. Every animal had an idea, but no one guessed what it was. So, they decided to send an elephant to find Judge Rabbit, who knew so much.

Elephant soon found Judge Rabbit munching on cucumbers and said, "Judge Rabbit, a strange creature has come to the forest and we need your help."

"I'll come if you feed me bananas," replied Judge Rabbit.

Elephant agreed, and so Judge Rabbit rode proudly on the elephant, back to the others. When they arrived, the animals gathered round.

"Wise Judge Rabbit," they said. "Tell us what this creature is and what ***It*** will do."

By now, the men were awake and shivering in fright under the cover. Judge Rabbit went carefully to the creature under the cover. Judge Rabbit noticed the hidden shapes and recognized humans. He felt their fear and thought they seemed harmless, so he decided to help them.

Scratching his ear, he picked up a large leaf, one with worm holes in it. Holes that made designs like letters. Holding it, he jumped on to a stump and stretched up his ears.

"Hmmm," he said. "I have a message from the God Indrea. He sent this creature, the 'Yuki-Yuki' to earth."

"Rabbit," moaned the elephant. "My brain is not big, please tell me what a Yuki-Yuki is."

"Well," said the quick-thinking rabbit, "Yuki-Yuki means a creature that can kill anything in a second." As soon as they heard that, the animals all pushed and shoved to get away. Soon the forest was quiet again, and the two men felt brave enough to peek out. They saw Judge Rabbit sitting calmly nearby.

"Akun, akun," they said, thanking him again and again.

"You are welcome," he replied. "And when you see me again, just bring me a few bananas." The men happily agreed, and Judge Rabbit hopped away to play another trick. And that is why the Khmer people still say: ***He who turns the tongue turns the world.***

Khmer *pronounced KAHMAY*

Telling Tips for "Judge Rabbit and the Strange Creature"

Telling animal tales appeals to some tellers and not to others. Some tellers like to get into the animal characters; others prefer to simply tell about them. Do what feels best. If you want to portray Judge Rabbit, find a few good actions: straightening his long ears, munching with a rabbit's scrunched-up face, and showing his head dart back and forth.

When he reads the "letter," he has the attention of all the animals, so he can afford to take his time. You can too. Prepare to read, and slowly share the words. Then, in contrast, you can speed up the part where the animals run away in fright. If you'd like to use your hands to show the fleeing animals, make your hands slither snakelike, fly like birds, and pounce away like the tiger.

During most of this time, whenever you mention the two men under the cloth, show their fright using your voice, or your face. At the end, show them coming ***very*** slowly out from under their covers. Finish with their obvious relief and thanks.

Activities

1. Since Judge Rabbit is such a popular character, he deserves a web site. Design a site to introduce him to the world. Include images, a description, stories, perhaps even a game or puzzle, as well as links to Cambodia and to other tricksters.
2. Rabbits are tricksters in many cultures. One of the most well known rabbit tricksters is, of course, Brer Rabbit. Go over some Brer Rabbit tales in the resources below. Then, make a Venn diagram to show how Judge Rabbit and Brer Rabbit are similar and different.

Resources

Parks, V. D. *Jump Again! More Adventures of Brer Rabbit.* Harcourt Brace, 1987. This book, followed by *Jump on Over*!, contains a range of Brer Rabbit tales.

Spagnoli, Cathy. *Judge Rabbit and the Tree Spirit.* Children's Book Press, 1993. Judge Rabbit helps some people after a human judge cannot decide their case.

———. *Judge Rabbit Helps the Fish.* The Wright Group, 1995. Judge Rabbit tricks large animals to help the weaker ones.

Philippines

"Marcella and the King"

In the Philippines, with so many languages and cultures, there are numerous regional tricksters. One known in certain parts is Juan Pusong. Similar to many male tricksters, he fools those in authority: the king, a sea captain, his family, and more.

But to be fair to females, the tale of the clever Marcella is given here. This is a popular tale of a girl who uses her brain to help her family and to outwit the king.

Marcella and the King

Long ago in the Philippines, lived clever Marcella. Her father was an advisor to the king. But it was Marcella who advised her father.

One day, the king decided to test her wit. He sent a small turkey to her, with a royal message, "You must prepare 20 different dishes from this one bird. At once!"

Marcella was sewing when the order came. She sat silently thinking for a few moments.

"Give this to the king with my compliments," she said, handing a needle to the messenger. "Tell him that as soon as he makes 20 spoons out of one needle, I will make 20 dishes out of one bird."

With hidden smiles, the messenger reported her words.

"A clever answer indeed," thought the king, and decided to test her again. Early the next morning, he sent a sheep to her, with a royal order, "You must sell this sheep today, then tonight return both the money and the sheep."

Marcella pondered the problem as she picked coconuts. Then she used her largest scissors to shear the thick wool from the sheep. She sold it for a good price.

In the evening, she brought the bare sheep and money to the palace. The king was now both pleased and annoyed—pleased to see such intelligence, but annoyed that he'd been outwitted.

"I shall give her one final challenge," he decided, then said to his servant, "Tell her that I am ill. And to cure me, I need a cup of bull's milk by tomorrow."

When Marcella heard this impossible command, she grew worried.

That night, she told her father of the king's demand.

"What can we do?" he sighed. "Just admit defeat when he returns from the river tomorrow."

"And why is he going there?" asked Marcella.

"To perform a special ceremony. So special, that no one is allowed near the river at that time," replied her father.

As Marcella listened, she suddenly had an idea. The next day, she went to the river just as the king approached. She bent down and washed her clothes.

Soon, her soap bubbles drifted to the king. Outraged, he sent his guards to fetch her.

"How dare you wash clothes here at this time?" he roared. "Didn't you hear my orders?"

"Yes, your majesty," she replied calmly."But, I needed a clean cloth to wrap round a baby, for my uncle just gave birth to a lovely boy."

"Foolish girl," said the king, "That's ridiculous. Men can never give birth."

"Very true, sir," she said. "Just as bulls can never give milk."

The king smiled in defeat, admiring Marcella's wit, wisdom, and courage. He rewarded her with gold and gems. Months later, a marriage was arranged to his son, the new king.

A fine wedding was held. And although she was far more clever than her husband, the two ruled well together. Thus everyone lived in peace and happiness for a long, long time.

Telling Tips for "Marcella and the King"

This is a little longer tale, with three separate incidents to share. Take enough time to learn it well, so that you can tell the whole story smoothly. And if you do forget an important detail, try to gently go back and add it in. It is best to act as if nothing happened when you make a mistake; or, if it is a big mistake, try to use humor to help listeners understand.

Activities

1. Hunt down some examples of clever girls from various cultures and make a colorful chart listing information about them. Include details about:
   - country or culture
   - appearance
   - personality
   - age
   - types of tricks played/problems solved
   - reaction of others in the story.

2. Since there are several different scenes in this story, it would make a nice picture book. But since it comes from Southeast Asia, you could try a technique found in some countries there: words and designs made on bamboo tubes. You probably don't have the big, wide bamboo needed, so use an oatmeal box or large coffee can. Measure the sides and find a piece of paper that fits nicely all around the box or can. Illustrate the story, in sequence, adding words as desired. When finished, attach the paper to the tube and share your tale. (You can also use stiff paper or cardboard that rolls into a tube and holds the shape by itself.)

Resources

Spagnoli, Cathy. *A Treasury of Asian Stories and Activities for Schools and Libraries.* Alleyside, 1998. Includes a tellable tale of the trickster Juan Pusong.

Wyndham, Robert. *Tales the People Tell in China.* Julian Messner, 1971. Includes a lovely variant of this clever girl tale.

Yolen, Jane. *Not One Damsel in Distress: World Folktales For Strong Girls.* Harcourt/Silver Whistle, 2000.

Chapter 22

Cambodia

"A-Chey Obeys His Master"

It is quite amazing that in a country with so much tragedy, we find several wonderful, funny tricksters. Both A-Chey and Judge Rabbit are well-known and admired in Cambodia and amidst Cambodian refugees. A-Chey begins his tricks as a young boy, fooled by a master. He quickly takes revenge on this master again and again. He is finally gifted to the King of Cambodia, but manages to trick him as well. After a series of tricks, the king, too, is fed up, and A-Chey is sent to China, where he tricks even the Emperor himself. After that, he is sent to a prison and tricks his way out; then he is sent back home, well-rewarded. He finally settles down somewhat, but continues playing tricks through his old age, even leaving one trick behind for after he has died.

A-Chey *pronounced A-CHAY*

Although A-Chey was never a slave, he was a servant who tricked his master. In that way, he can be compared to High John the Conqueror, the African-American slave trickster who played tricks on his master.

A-Chey Obeys His Master

In Cambodia long ago lived clever A-Chey. He lived by his quick wits, fooling those who were older, bigger, and stronger. As a boy, he worked for a rich landlord and played many a trick on him, too.

One day, the landlord's wife sent for A-Chey and said, "Go to the royal court. Tell your master that his dinner awaits him." A-Chey ran out shouting, "Master, come eat! Master, come eat!" As he raced to the court, his calls became louder still.

In the royal court, the landlord and the other noblemen tried to ignore A-Chey's noise. But the sound grew and grew until no one could do any work. Then right outside the door came a roar, ***"Master, time to come! Hurry and eat now!"***

Hiding his anger, the master bowed and left the court. Outside, he spoke furiously to A-Chey, "If you are ever sent to call me again, you fool, never yell so loudly! I am not a water buffalo in the field. Next time, come very slowly and politely up to me. Stand and wait until I order you to speak. Then whisper your message."

"Was my voice too loud, sir? Forgive me. Next time I will do just as you say," said A-Chey, hiding a smile. They returned home for a peaceful few days. But the next week, when the master was at court again, his fine house suddenly began to burn.

"A-Chey," ordered the wife, "go tell your master about the fire. Bring him back at once." But A-Chey didn't hurry, he walked slowly to the court, exactly as the landlord had commanded. With small steps, he moved up to his master. Then he stood, waiting. To teach him a lesson, the master ignored A-Chey for a long time. Finally, the master ordered him to speak. A-Chey whispered too softly, "Your house is on fire, sir."

"Speak up, fool," demanded the master.

"Your house is on fire, sir," repeated A-Chey in a hushed tone.

"I can't hear you," fumed the master. ***"Louder!"***

"Your house is on fire, sir."

"What?" cried the master. "Why didn't you cry out right away?"

"I just followed your orders, sir," replied a pleased A-Chey.

"Fool! Hurry home and save anything light and valuable," commanded the angry master.

A-Chey raced back and into the burning house. He came out with his arms full. Soon after, the master returned to see his house almost destroyed.

"Well, at least you had time to save something," he said. "Show me what."

A-Chey proudly displayed several birds' nests of sticks, straw, and feathers.

"A-Chey!" shouted the master. "I said to save anything light and valuable. This is junk."

"But, sir, these are very light, just as you ordered," replied the clever A-Chey. "And most valuable to birds, too." The master scowled and walked off, fooled again.

Telling Tips for "A-Chey Obeys His Master"

Decide how to show A-Chey's age: remember, he is a young but confident boy. Make the master quite proud and vain. Show how loud and rude A-Chey's first cries are. Then, with the fire, bring out the contrast between the whispered words of A-Chey, which grow slowly louder, and the master's anger. At the end, when he brings out the light things, try to show the many sides of A-Chey: he knows he fooled his master, but he can't show it; he has to appear very innocent and rather foolish, although he is actually very clever. If you like to act, you can show A-Chey running into the house, with arms waving away smoke, etc. But don't get too carried away or you may lose your audience.

Activities

1. A-Chey was a very inventive young man. In one of his later stories, he invents a certain kind of noodle, and uses them to see the Chinese Emperor's face! Use your ability to invent. Dream up the kind of invention A-Chey might make to save himself work while on a farm:
   - putting out a fire
   - feeding pigs and horses
   - guarding the garden, etc.
2. A-Chey loved to trick his master by taking his time. Make a maze of the master's burned house. Plan in two routes: 1) a round-about route from inside to out, which A-Chey would take if ordered, and 2) the fastest route, which he would take on his own.

Resources

Goldberg, Rube. *The Best of Rube Goldberg.* Prentice-Hall, 1979. A great collection of zany inventions.

Sanfield, Steve. *The Adventures of High John the Conqueror.* Franklin Watts, 1989. A fine selection of tales about this African-American slave trickster.

Japan

"Oiko the Strong"

Japan has a large variety of tricksters, some quite well-known outside of Japan, others not. Since regional stories, often told in dialect, are well-loved and known in Japan, many regions have their own tricksters. From Shigejiro in northern Hokkaido to Kichomu in southern Kyushu, there are numerous local tricksters. Another favorite, now more widely known through comics and TV, is the young novice priest, Ikkyusan.

Animal tricksters are also popular: Kitsune the fox, and Tanuki the badger are the most popular. Resources to find some of these tricksters follow below. But the next story highlights a rather unique female character: a super-strong woman who

Oiko the Strong

Mukashi, mukashi...

Ishibashi *pronounced EE-SHE-BAH-SHE*

Oiko *pronounced OH-EE-KOE*

Long ago in Ishibashi village, Oiko a very strong woman, once lived. How strong? I shall tell you.

One dry year, some people in Ishibashi village tricked her.

They built a dam that kept water from her fields. Oiko's rice plants began to wilt, and they cried in thirst.

She soon found out why, and although angry, she used her wits and her strength to fight back.

In the middle of the night, she tiptoed outside to a ***huge*** rock. It was as large as a horse, and many times as heavy.

But Oiko lifted it easily, as if it were made from a spider's web.

dobon *pronounced DOE-BONE (This is the sound of the rock dropping into the river.)*

Holding the rock on her head, she ran and dropped it in the river—***dobon!***—to stop everyone else's water. Then she returned home and slept peacefully.

In the morning, the farmers went to work, saw their fields strangely dry, and wondered why. They raced to the river, and their jaws dropped.

A very, very large rock sat right in the middle…blocking all their water.

"Oiko did this, only she could. We must take it away," they cried. And they tried and tried. Grunting, groaning men filled the riverbed, struggling to free the rock.

Yoisho *pronounced YO-EE-SHOW*

Yoisho, Yoisho...they pushed and pushed and pushed. But that rock only stayed still. Soon more villagers came, trampling the nearby fields, trying to help. They pushed the men who pushed the rock. But that enormous rock just sat and never moved.

"We must ask Oiko to forgive us and help us," everyone finally agreed. They dashed to her house. They fell to the ground before her, like flattened bugs, pleading.

"Forgive us," they begged. "We'll tear down the dam. Please move that rock."

Now Oiko was not a mean woman. So when they swore never to trick her again, she promised to help. Yet she was not one to show off. She waited until the moon smiled in the dark, then she walked to the river, and quickly picked up the rock. She shook it to remove the water and carried it on her head to a field far away.

There she dropped it and there it stays to this day, the great boulder known as Oiko's watermouth rock.

Telling Tips for "Oiko the Strong"

Use mime if you like to show just how strong Oiko is. And you can make the farmers look especially sorry and pitiful when they are begging for her forgiveness. Japanese tellers often use delightful sounding words; their language is especially rich in such sounds. Use the Japanese words included in the tale here; they add a nice touch. And since many of the sounds accompany movement—pushing, pulling, lifting—add your own sounds of physical effort.

Activities

1. The role of a superstrong woman trickster is very unusual. Can you think of others? In small groups, develop her character and make up at least one more tall tale type of trick that shows her strength. Place a large piece of paper on the table with Oiko in the center. Each group then draws and writes a brief description of their trick, each placed around the center character, making a powerful mural.
2. Imagine you were sent by a newspaper to interview Oiko. What types of questions would you ask such an unusual character? If time allows, write the whole interview, including her answers.

Resources

Dorson, Richard. *Folk Legends of Japan.* Tuttle, 1981. A well known folklorist shares a number of trickster tales in this varied collection.

Osborne, Mary. *American Tall Tales.* Knopf, 1991. Tall tales of strength told in the United States.

Yanagita, Kunio. *The Yanagita Kunio Guide to the Japanese Folk Tale.* Translated by Fanny Hagin Mayer. Indiana University Press, 1986. This rich sourcebook of Japanese plots includes many tales of strength and tricks.

Vietnam

"The Horses"

In this story, the trick seems to be played not only on the three boys, but on the listener as well. It is a delightful problem tale. Since it is difficult to figure out why it works, some students may take it home to puzzle over. Such math tricks and puzzles are found around the globe. For centuries, small stories were used to teach logic and problem solving, in many cultures. Yet in a society which values learning, as in Vietnam, they are perhaps even more common, as is the role of the wise teacher.

The Horses

Once in Vietnam, there lived a man and his three sons. It was a happy family, and one where scholarship was much valued. The boys went to a small village school with a wise teacher. Many peaceful years passed, until the father took ill and began to fade away. On his deathbed, he called to his sons.

"My sons," he sighed, "you have been kind and loving sons to me. I have enjoyed a good life and I know that you will care for my spirit after my death. Now, before I die, I wish to divide my property."

The man slowly told them how to divide the household utensils, his lands, and finally, his animals. He ended with instructions about his horses. "I wish my eldest son to have ½ of my horses, the second son to have ⅓, and the third son to have ⅙."

After these words, the father died, well-satisfied.

Arrangements were made for a fine funeral and the property was soon divided among the sons, except for the horses. Because the man had 17 horses. And none of the boys knew how to divide 17 by ½, ⅓, and ⅙.

After much useless debate, they decided to ask their wise teacher. They ran to him and told him of their problem. He immediately smiled and said he could help them.

(Storytellers: Stop and ask the audience for a solution. If the right answer is given, smile and retell it for all to hear; if wrong ones come up, praise the efforts and go on to give the solution.)

"I will give you one of my horses," he said. "Now, how many horses do you have?"

"18," replied the boys.

"And can you divide 18 by ½, ⅓, and ⅙?" asked the teacher.

"Yes, easily," the boys answered.

"So, eldest son, you will get ½ of 18. How many is that?"

"Nine," replied the boy.

"And second son, you will receive ⅓ of 18, which is...?"

"Six, sir," said the boy.

"Good, then, last son, you will get ⅙ of 18. How many horses will that be?"

"Two," answered the son.

"Now, let us add your horses, just to check," suggested the teacher.

"9 and 6 = 15 plus 2 = 17," said the eldest son.

"Good," beamed the teacher, "so you don't need my horse." And he took back his horse with a smile.

Telling Tips for "The Horses"

This is a simple tale and can be told simply. However, be sure to know the fractions very well. Don't get confused and have the boys get different shares... the story won't work out!

Perhaps you'll want to show the division of goods by moving your hands to mime what goes to each son. You might like to show the age of the teacher by stroking a long beard. Go over the last part, with math, quite slowly, to make sure your listeners follow the arithmetic. Pause briefly to let them answer if you wish (as indicated in the story script). And at the end, as you say the last line, you can "take back" your horse by pulling its imaginary rope. That adds humor to the surprise last line.

Activities

1. For centuries, stories have been used to sharpen wits. There are numbers of stories with math tricks and problems in them. Use the resources below to find other math tales. Then have each student write just one page, with an illustration. Duplicate each page, bind, and you will have a class *Tricky Math Tales* book, which will appeal to a range of readers and tellers. Give copies to other classes, and make sure your library gets a copy!
2. In older times, and even today, many villages around the world have an elder or several elders known for their wisdom and experience. The boys in this story took their problem to such an elder. Divide into groups and have each group imagine a small village, somewhere in the world, in any time period. Then together:

- create a wise elder
- describe him/her
- decide who brings the elder a problem
- tell what the problem is
- show how he or she solves it.

Resources

Mathemagic *www.scri.fsu.edu/~dennisl/cms/activity/math_magic.html*

Good site for a variety of math challenges.

Shannon, George. *Stories to Solve.* Greenwillow Books, 1985. The first in a fine series, rich in problem-solving challenges.

Chapter 25

Japan

"A Fox's Tricks?"

This is an unusual tale, since it is a trick which a fox trickster would play, but it is played here by a human. Kitsune the fox is often found in dark places, or pretending to be a human. Often, the fox disguises herself as a lovely lady, sometimes given away by the fox tail peaking out of her kimono. The fox can play very nice tricks as well as mischievous ones. At times, the fox can comfort humans and help them. At other times, it can make fools of humans—giving them coins that are really leaves, or transforming itself. The fox is also well-known as a trickster figure in Chinese and Korean lore.

In this popular tale, a clever human borrows fox legends to save himself. He uses his skill as an actor to pretend to be a fox changing shapes. Thus, perhaps, he reminds listeners how they, too, can borrow the skills of the trickster to get out of all kinds of trouble.

A Fox's Tricks?

Mukashi, mukashi...

Long ago in Tokyo an actor named Kusaku once lived. He was a fine actor, but he wanted to become even better. So he found a teacher who could give him voice exercises, eye exercises, finger exercises, and tell him many tales.

But one day in class, Kusaku started to cry as he read a letter. His teacher was angry and shouted, "You are not to read letters in class!" But since he was a kind man, he then asked, "And why are you crying?"

"Gomen kudasai, I'm sorry," Kusaku sobbed. "This is a letter from my mother. She is very sick and may die, so she wrote to say good-bye."

"You must go see her," his teacher declared. "And since you're an actor, take your costumes and make-up, too!"

"Domo arigato, thank you, thank you," cried Kusaku. Then he packed quickly and ran, *pakapan, pakapan,* toward his mother.

When he was close to home, he stopped for green tea. As he started to leave, the old woman there said, "Wait! Wait! Are you going over the mountain now?"

"Yes," said Kusaku.

"Alone? In the dark?" she asked.

"Y-e-s," replied Kusaku.

Uwabami *pronounced OO-WA-BAH-ME*

"Aren't you afraid of the uwabami?"

"The what?" asked Kusaku.

"The uwabami!"

"The who?"

"The uwabami!" she shouted.

And then she told him of the uwabami, a fierce python that lived on the mountain, who liked to change shapes and munch on human bones.

doki *pronounced DOE-KEY*

Now, Kusaku was not very brave, but he did love his mother. So he went slowly up the lonely mountain, his heart beating, "doki, doki, doki."

Every time he saw a dark shadow he thought, "Ooooooo, I hope that's not the uwabami."

And every time he heard a new sound, he thought, "Ooooooo, I hope ***that's*** not the uwabami!"

Just then, an old man appeared next to him.

"Oh, I'm glad you're here," said Kusaku. "They say there's a python monster here, but now together we can beat him up."

On and on he kept talking nervously. And he didn't notice that the old man wasn't listening. Instead, he was licking his hungry lips.

"Ahhhh," thought Kusaku as he suddenly saw a lick. "Maybe he is the uwabami!"

"Yessss, I am the uwabami," shouted the old man suddenly, "and I'm going to eat you **up**!"

"No, you wouldn't want to," cried Kusaku, remembering his grandmother's stories about foxes that could change shapes.

"Why not! I love human flesh!" cried the uwabami.

"Yes, but I'm not a human being, I'm a fox!" Kusaku answered.

"Ugh, I hate fox meat," the old man groaned. "But prove it! Turn into something else, the way a fox could."

Kusaku slipped behind a tree and slapped on make-up and a costume. All at once, a mighty warrior appeared, holding a sword.

"Now, something else!" barked the uwabami.

Kusaku disappeared again to change his make-up and kimono. Suddenly, an elegant lady pranced out, saying, "Kon ban wa."

"Once more!" ordered the python. Luckily, Kusaku had one more costume left. ***So***… in moments, a young student walked out, reading a book.

"Yes, you are a fox, I won't eat you," said the uwabami. Then the two walked together in peace. Soon Kusaku had another idea and said,

"Now that we're almost friends, let's share secrets. Let's tell each other what we're most afraid of in the whole world. I'll start. I am so, so, so scared of ***gold***."

"That doesn't scare me at all," bragged the uwabami, "but I am terrified of hot tobacco juice."

Just then, the sun smiled, and the night fled. Kusaku saw his village and ran off with a wave. Soon, he was home happily with his mother. Every day, he made her fine soups, and soon she was much stronger.

It was time now to return to Tokyo. But first, Kusaku wanted to help his friends, for they lived in great fear of the uwabami.

"I know what he's afraid of," Kusaku told the villagers. "At sunset, come here and bring tobacco, and big pots."

Soon, fires were lit and the tobacco juice started to boil. When the mixture was ready, the villagers ran up to the uwabami's cave. They threw it all over the entrance.

"Aaaahhh!" came a roar as the uwabami, who was scared, changed from one shape to another. At last, he came out as a huge and powerful python.

"Aaarraaa!" he growled, "now I must leave, since everyone knows my ssssecret. But I know Kusaku's, too. I'll get back at him before I go!"

Quickly, he gathered gold, much gold, then slithered, "***zuru, zuru, zuru***," onto Kusaku's roof. With angry thrusts, he poured the gold down the chimney, crying, ***"Die! Die! Die!"***

But of course Kusaku was not scared at all. His face wore a ***huge*** smile as he counted the coins tumbling down. Soon, a great pile sparkled on the floor.

Early the next morning, Kusaku divided the gold into four parts. He gave some to his mother, and some to his friends.

He kept some for his teacher, and some for himself—to buy a new costume or two!

Then, with a big ***"Sayonara,"*** he waved good-bye and went back to live happily in Tokyo.

Telling Tips for "A Fox's Tricks?"

This tale may be the hardest one in the book to tell. It is also the longest, with a number of Japanese sound words. Use your voice to frighten listeners when Kusaku starts walking up the mountain and hears noises. Try the storyteller's trick of lowering your voice slightly right before you shout, ***"Yes! I am the uwabami!"*** Show Kusaku's changes: pose like a warrior, next act a bit like a lady, then like a young boy.

The story has fine dialogue, so if you feel comfortable, go back and forth in different voices between Kusaku and the 1) teacher, 2) old woman, and 3) uwabami. You can also cut out some of this dialogue and just describe the exchange.

If you'd like a good prop, try using **kamishibai**, the Japanese storytelling cards (see instructions in the activity section). When you practice with them, watch for the following:

- don't let your hands get in the way of the kamishibai
- make sure the cards aren't shaking back and forth or vibrating
- avoid looking at kamishibai and not at audience
- make sure your voice doesn't get too quiet

There may be a need to edit the story length; you don't want a story that rambles, nor one that whizzes by (let the cards help pace the story).

Activities

1. To make kamishibai, take about eight cards of manila tagboard or stiff paper, cut roughly to 6" x 9".

   Quickly sketch out eight important scenes from the story, either on newsprint or directly on the cards.

   After the sequence is finished, make bold, colorful drawings for each scene, using markers, paints, and crayons. Make them big enough for the audience to see.

   Number each card on the back, then practice telling to other students in small groups. Hold cards chest high, directly facing the audience. After several practice sessions, use kamishibai to tell the story to other classes in the school.
2. Although this tale is a popular one in Japan, a Seattle zoo worker felt that it portrayed pythons in an unfair way. As a class, decide whether the tale should be changed to make the snake less of a negative stereotype. Discuss whether fiction changed fact too much in this tale. Consider why.

Resources

Bender, Lionel. *Pythons and Boas.* Gloucester, 1988. Introduces several types of constrictor snakes.

Hastings, Selina. *Reynard, the Fox.* Tambourine Books, 1991. Here is a fine collection of tales about a European fox trickster, who doesn't change shapes the way Asian foxes do.

Part 3

More Ideas and Resources

Telling Beyond the Book

A Few More Ideas

By sharing the ideas and stories in this book, you've nourished the fine art of storytelling and the clever art of the trickster! Use the following ideas and resources to keep you telling and telling.

Exhibits, Festivals, and Swaps

Host a friendly story swap for parents and students, elders, and librarians. Encourage people to bring a small story, and perhaps a snack to share. When you're ready to expand, plan a storytelling festival in a school, community center, library, or park to share stories with a wider audience.

Taping Tales

If resources allow, consider taping tales on cassette, on the radio, or over the Internet. Students can work in small groups to perfect their individual tales. Use feedback sheets which emphasize oral telling—without gestures—having students check: imagery used, voice sounds and feeling, character voices, sound effects, story length, pauses, nervous vocalizations (uhs, ahs, you-knows).

Do several practice tapes and then make a good quality finished product (you might even be able to tape at a local radio station). If you are really serious, have students design a tape cover, then duplicate cassette copies to sell as a fundraiser or for distribution to museums, libraries, hospitals, or sister schools.

Students can also make a storytelling videotape, following the process of practice, feedback, taping, and viewing. Perhaps you can get some storytelling taped by a local cable TV station. Since gestures become very important in front of the camera, have students choose from the beginning if they want the security of a chair or if they will stand. Creative settings, props, and bits of background music can also add to a video story tape.

Storytelling Club

Storytelling is an art, and some students may be truly drawn to it. A storytelling club or storytelling troupe is an excellent way to keep the excitement going for these students, helping them to further refine their skills. There is much chance for feedback and support in such small groups; students will feel free to take chances and try new materials in such a warm, nonthreatening atmosphere. Students can expand their repertoire of tales and find new places to tell: bookstores, youth groups, business clubs, libraries, museums, neighboring schools, retirement homes, day care centers, and more.

A Few More Resources on Storytelling

Bauer, Caroline Feller. *Caroline Feller Bauer's New Handbook for Storytellers.* American Library Association, 1993.

de Vos, Gail. *Storytelling for Young Adults.* Libraries Unlimited, 1991.

Folktales of the World series, University of Chicago Press.

Lipman, Doug. *The Storytelling Coach: How to Listen, Praise, and Bring Out People's Best.* August House, 1995.

Livo, Norma and S. Rietz. *Storytelling Folklore Sourcebook.* Libraries Unlimited, 1991.

MacDonald, Margaret Read. *The Storyteller's Sourcebook.* Neal-Schuman/Gale Research, 1982.

Pellowski, Anne. *The World of Storytelling.* H. W. Wilson, 1990.

World Folklore Series, Libraries Unlimited.

Trickster Tale Sources and Resources

Sources for Stories

Below, you'll find the sources for these trickster tales as well as a few more of the many other resources available on tricksters.

"The Missing Ticket" I heard in Singapore from a student at one of my storytelling programs, 1999.

"A Long Tale" was shared in a storytelling workshop by a number of Chinese teachers, Singapore, 1999.

"A Fine Moon" I heard from Park Young Ok, Seoul, 1995.

"Jump In" and "The Painting Contest" came to me from a teacher in Bellevue, WA, who heard them from her Thai husband, 1991.

"On the Farm" and "Your Thoughts" were told to me by a group of Lao women at the Refugee Women's Alliance, Seattle, 1988.

"Agu Tompa Borrows a Pot" was collected in Dharamsala, India, from Tibetan refugees, 1975; it is also found in Rinjing Dorje's excellent book, *Uncle Tompa*, published by Station Hill Arts, and adapted with his kind permission.

"To Trick a Thief" comes from an afternoon of story swapping at a great teahouse in Singapore, 1998.

"A Fair Trade" is a Burmese law tale, found in Aung's *Burmese Law Tales* and as the Kuta-Vanija-Jataka in India.

"Sang Kanchil and the Lion" and "The Stolen Scents" I heard from Nurmala, a young listener at Borders Bookstore, Singapore, 1998.

"Why the Water Buffalo Can't Talk" and "The Horses" were told to me at the Refugee Women's Alliance, Seattle, by Emanuelle Chi Dang, 1990.

"The Farmer and the Tokaebi" was told to me in a children's library in Pusan, Korea, by 10-year-old Park Yong-hi, 1995.

"Monkey Thieves" I heard from Blia Xiong in Seattle, 1987.

"The Well" was collected from K. S. Gopal, in 1979, at Cholamandal Artists' Village, Chennai, India.

"A Goblin's Trick" was collected from Ratna Soonder Shakya in Kathmandu by Daya Shakya, and used with her kind permission.

"A Strange Bird" was told to me in Bali, 1977, by Robbi, an Indonesian friend.

"Lazy Dragon at the Inn" I adapted from Yang's *The Courtesan's Jewel Box.*

"Trust" came from Sultan Ali, Cholamandal, India, 1977.

"Judge Rabbit and the Strange Creature" and "A-Chey Obeys His Master" were collected in 1990 from Lina Mao Wall and others at the Refugee Women's Alliance, Seattle, and from Putha Touche, Seattle.

"Marcella and the King" is adapted from M. Mariano's *Tales of the Philippines.* Sterling, 1982.

"Oiko the Strong" was shared by Shugi Ahiko in Yokohama, Japan, 1985.

"A Fox's Tricks?" was told by various tellers in Japan, 1991.

A Few More Tricks

Aardema, Verna. *Borreguita and the Coyote: A Tale From Ayutla, Mexico.* Alfred A. Knopf, 1991.

Bryan, Ashley. *The Dancing Granny.* Macmillan, 1987.

Ginsburg, M. *One Trick Too Many: Fox Stories From Russia.* Dial, 1973.

Gleeson, B. *Anansi.* Picture Book Studio, 1992.

Goble, Paul. *Iktomi and the Buffalo Skull.* Orchard, 1991.

Goss, Linda and Clay Goss. *Jump Up and Say: A Collection of Black Storytelling.* Simon & Schuster, 1995.

Haley, Gail. *Mountain Jack Tales.* Dutton, 1992.

Jones, H. *Coyote Tales.* Holt, Rinehart & Winston, 1971.

Kimmel, Eric. *The Adventures of Hershel of Ostropol.* Holiday House, 1995.

Kimmel, Eric. *Anansi and the Talking Melon.* Holiday House, 1994.

Laughing Together. National Book Trust, 1991.

Lester, J. *The Tales of Uncle Remus: The Adventures of Brer Rabbit.* Dial, 1987.

Mayo, G. W. *Meet Tricky Coyote!* Walker, 1993.

McDermott, Gerald. *Coyote.* Harcourt Brace, 1994.

Robinson, G. *Raven the Trickster.* Atheneum, 1982.

Thompson, Vivian. *Hawaiian Legends of Tricksters and Riddlers.* Holiday House, 1969.

Williams, J. *The Wicked Tricks of Tyl Uilenspiegel.* Four Winds, 1978.

Williams, J. S. *Maui Goes Fishing.* The University of Hawaii Press, 1991.